Hungry
as we are

A CELEBRATION OF 20 YEARS OF PUBLISHING

An anthology
of Washington
area poets

Hungry
as we are

EDITED BY
ANN DARR

THE WASHINGTON WRITERS' PUBLISHING HOUSE
WASHINGTON, D.C.

First edition 1995.
Printed in the United States of America.

Design by Jeanne Krohn
Typesetting by Barbara Shaw
Printing by McNaughton & Gunn

Library of Congress Cataloging-in-Publication Data
Hungry as we are : an anthology of Washington area poets / edited by
    Ann Darr. —1st ed.
        p.   cm.
    ISBN 0-931846-48-X
    1. American poetry—Washington Metropolitan Area. 2. American
    poetry—Washington (D.C.) 3. American poetry—20th century.
    I. Darr, Ann. II. Title: A celebration of 20 years of publishing
    PS548.D6H86   1995
    811'.50809753—dc20   95-40882
                                                               CIP

WASHINGTON WRITERS' PUBLISHING HOUSE
P.O. Box 15271
Washington, D.C. 20003

HUNGRY AS WE ARE
An Anthology of Washington Area Poets

Ann Darr, *Editor*
Laurie Stroblas, *Editorial Coordinator*
Ann B. Knox, *Production Coordinator*
Jeanne Krohn, *Graphic Designer*

FIRST READERS

Barri Armitage   Shirley G. Cochrane   Martin Galvin
Laurie Stroblas   Joseph C. Thackery   Elaine M. Upton

SECOND READERS

Grace Cavalieri   Maxine Clair   Ann B. Knox

THIRD READERS

Nan Fry   Patricia G. Garfinkel
Barbara F. Lefcowitz   Elaine Magarrell

SPECIAL ASSISTANCE FROM

Laura Brylawski-Miller   Elizabeth Follin-Jones
Patricia G. Garfinkel   Jean Johnson
E. Ethelbert Miller   Jean Nordhaus
Betty Parry

Our gratitude to the many WWPH poets and those in the community who provided invaluable help with this anthology during the past two years. We thank **Dan Johnson** for his acknowledgments acumen; **Kim Roberts** for her bravura biographical notes; **Ann B. Knox** for her production prowess; **Jeanne Krohn** for many years of gracious graphic design; **Barbara Shaw** for her on-target typesetting; and **Grace Cavalieri** for her look back at the early days and development of the press. Special thanks to **Laurie Stroblas** and **Ann Darr** for their ceaseless efforts, displaying expertise and energy during the ongoing editorial process. Finally, we are grateful for funding support from the Max and Victoria Dreyfus Foundation, the Eugene and Agnes E. Meyer Foundation, the Jenny McKean Moore Fund for Writers, the Prince Charitable Trusts, and donations from the many Friends of Washington Writers' Publishing House, as well as project funding in part from the D.C. Commission on the Arts and the National Endowment for the Arts.

—The Washington Writers' Publishing House

On behalf of The Washington Writers' Publishing House, I
am grateful to all the poets who assisted the challenging process
of reading poems submitted for consideration and in preparing
this anthology. Open call for poems from writers within a 60-mile
radius of Washington, D.C., including Baltimore, netted more
that 800 poems. These were pared to an expressive collection of
poems by 122 poets.

I especially want to thank Laurie Stroblas, who served as
literary cardiologist with patience and enthusiasm all the way.

Organizing a diverse selection of poems is an intuitive act,
one I cannot plan for in advance. Rather, I see what is there, and
the book simply begins to materialize. Or, not so simply.

Editing an anthology involves the same creative energy that
goes into writing a poem. There is the same depth of concentra-
tion, the same intense focusing. It is as mysterious a process for
me as is making a poem. I have edited about two dozen poetry
manuscripts over the years for friends and colleagues. Each time
I approach a new set of poems I'm not sure I'll be successful.
I really do not know what made it possible for me to organize all
these poems by such varied voices. Fortunately, so much richness
was here that natural divisions began to stand out.

I started with the most obvious of categories—food, love,
sex—the ones I hope readers will also begin with. The heart of
each poem that fit these categories was quite visible. But then
there were the others, those more elusive, those with twin hearts,
duplicitous hearts, those with hidden chambers, those that
seemed heartless.

I added more categories.

Kinship. Loss. Nostalgia. Deprivation. Art. Physicality. Travel.
Spirituality. Politics. Meaning. Soon the poems themselves
provided inspiration for section titles. The heart of each section
declared itself loud and clear.

There are 210 poems that hungrily await you here.

Ann Darr

FOREWORD

BY E. ETHELBERT MILLER

I am broke and hungry
ragged and dirty too
I said I'm broke and hungry
ragged and dirty too
Mama, if I clean up can
I go home with you

—*Blind Lemon Jefferson*

Quite often when one speaks of hunger, one speaks of space, a space that can be physical, emotional, or spiritual. The empty space in one's stomach or heart. My mother, whenever she spoke of hunger, would think first of the Great Depression and then of the food on my plate. This was how I was raised, to be thankful for God's blessings. Years later I would think of hunger and its relationship to writing and the searching for the correct word and the satisfaction felt when a poem or story was completed.

Yet, my own hunger has too often been interwoven with desire and a longing to touch, to hold and be held. How many times have you looked into a woman's or man's eyes for answers, only to discover that it is the blues you are sitting across from?

Yes, the blues is metaphor for hunger.

It is ironic that this anthology finds its birth and origins in the Washington, D.C., area, a place known for the production of paper and not wheat, corn, or potatoes.

As I write this introduction, our political leaders have undertaken a serious debate about the role of government in our society. We seem to be moving into the next century with a new and cavalier disregard for the poor and the hungry, and for the support of art, too. Our proposed international policies advocate a new world isolationism, drawing narrow bounds for our generosity. We blame the media and information technology for making the world too small.

This collection of poems reflects the poet's world. Here is the hunger for meaning as well as the celebration of its attainment.

No emotion remains hidden, every desire is revealed. In Geraldine Connolly's "The Unexplained Territories," the poet begins seductively with:

> I eat poetry for breakfast
> in the pink and silver diner
> that floats atop a bank of the Susquehanna
> lifting crisp words like cereal
> into my mouth with sweetrolls and doughnuts...

Richard Peabody's "I'm in Love with the Morton Salt Girl" describes that moment of innocence and infatuation we all go through and yet the poem also hints at how everyday items attract us. All the works in this anthology are connected by a common fiber. Each poem comments on the next, every poet attempting to explain that space we define as hunger. "I let my hunger define me, / although, like so many men, / I didn't even know its name" are the sentiments of Kim Roberts in her poem "The Nameless."

There are many "hungers" in the book as suggested by its numerous sections. Barbara Goldberg wisely tells us

> The body decides
> since the body must answer
> to curious, various hungers.

In today's world it is the poet's heart that must remain large. It is the poet's words that must feed us if we are to live. It was Roque Dalton who wrote:

> I believe the world is beautiful
> and that poetry, like bread, is for everyone.

This collection is one wonderful loaf. Let us share it with our brothers and sisters, our friends, our neighbors, our lovers. Let this book chase those blues away...let it endure.

Memorial Day
May 28, 1995

FOOD

What hunger first saw this as food

LOVE

All we know of love

S E X

Flesh stirred to a touch

KINSHIP
The place I started from

LOSS
An unknown withered hour

NOSTALGIA
An undertow of dream and exile

DEPRIVATION
Hunger waits with time on its side

CONTENTS

CONTENTS

TRAVEL
Unexplained territories

SPIRITUALITY
Holy earth

CONTENTS

Hungry
as we are

What
hunger
first
saw this
as food

ARTICHOKE

*If poetry did not exist, would you
have had the wit to invent it?*
—Howard Nemerov

He had studied in private years ago
the way to eat these things, and was prepared
when she set the clipped green globe before him.
He only wondered (as he always did
when he plucked from the base the first thick leaf,
dipped it into the sauce and caught her eye
as he deftly set the velvet curve against
the inside edges of his lower teeth
and drew the tender pulp toward his tongue
while she made some predictable remark
about the sensuality of this act
then sheared away the spines and ate the heart)
what mind, what hunger, first saw this as food.

ADVICE TO A DAUGHTER

Do not gnaw chicken bones before
a lover, I tell her, as we crunch
the cartilage of a hapless hen.

Could put him off, give rise
to thoughts you might have
taste for more than skin.

My lover is so meticulous
he uses knife and fork,
misses deep pleasures.

I have to sneak to the kitchen,
chew both our drumsticks clean
before I scrape the plates.

The best is what some call
the parson's nose, others term
the pope's, the rabbi's.

My mother said: What scuttles
through the fence the last
is surely the most succulent.

So while our chicken stews apart
you and I retrieve the bubbling bones,
gnaw, and juices trickling down

our chins, weigh the risks of loss:
either a fastidious lover
or the choice parts of a bird.

APPETITES

Dein Zug kennt keinen Bahnhof,
my mother would tell me,
astonished at how much
I could consume of whatever
pleased me: ice cream or chocolates,
and later, smoked salmon, Westphalian ham.
Your train knows no station.
Now that I'm an adult, my train knows
several stations, though sometimes,
it's a greed express, ripping through
an entire apple tart,
a quart of blueberries,
a pound of Camembert.
All children are greedy
until they learn to curb unattractive habits,
like chewing fingernails or picking noses.
From Old English, *graedig*: Beowulf didn't worry
about how he looked chowing down
a leg of ox or a few pheasants, whole.
A friend taps his wife's frail wrist: *honey,*
wouldn't sorbet be better than ice cream?
Some trains idle and weeds then grow between their tracks.
Once for two weeks I ate nothing,
drinking only mineral water.
I imagined myself light as an airmail letter;
a man's hands could encircle my waist.
I climbed flights of stairs one at a time,
panting. The memory makes me see myself
stare at the shape of a woman
who swims in my pool: her thighs
have the heft of a good dictionary.

She's never sick,
she can lift a lawn mower over the hedge,
she's the only conductor on her train,
and she knows which stations
are worth stopping for.

BLUEBERRY WOMAN

The blueberry woman has wrecked her week
and the kitchen, baking muffins, baking pies.
She reeks of blueberry jam, has steeped herself
with thoughts of blood and bloody butcherings.
What she comes to at the end, and prints
in blue juice on the bathroom door,
is the family's menu for the harvest month.

Her children, home for lunch and stuffed
with chalk, a permanent peanutbutter glaze
to their eyes, are served up to their regret
grilled blueberries au gratin, blueberry soup,
blueberry tart in blueberry juice, then spooned
out the door and back to school, their faces
drained, their mouths as dyed as grief.

Her husband attachés his way from work, dulled
to boldness by drinks with the boys. What he
expects for dinner is baked potatoes,
New York Strip, asparagus with hollandaise.
He also expects the kids to be fed and bathed
and ready for bed and his wife dressed up
for dessert and ready, by god, to roll. She is.

She darkens up what is dull about the meal.
What he gets is blueberries a la carte.
Blueberry hash he gets and blueberry toast
and blueberry sauce for the blueberry mousse.
As he nods off in bed she leaves him lack
and blue. Dressed to kill, she heads outside.
A blue moon ripens in the letting sky.

In that new light, she murders what
she can, the strawberry beds,
the blueberry patch, rows and rows
of tomatoes. Come the next harvest,
her family can eat flowers, as far as she's
concerned. Roots they can eat, or seeds,
rainbows, daffodils, stripes of the blue moon.

MY MOTHER'S REFRIGERATOR

My mother's refrigerator opened,
white colossus stuffed with bundles
of meat and cheese, rows of jars,
dozens of oranges about to roll
out of a bag's red loops
onto the floor. There was a poverty
about its fullness. The more we took
from it, the more she gained. She rushed
to stuff another package of sweets
into the freezer. Here, she plies
our plates with unwanted potatoes.

The trip to table takes on a misery
of pleasure. Food accumulates:
ice cream and meatloaf, creamed mushrooms.
The counters fill with spices
and potholders, ornate serving pieces.
If we could knock down those engravings
of parsley and pear, if we could starve
the gods of unrealized ambition,
what space would remain, not this
frozen hold filled with the old country,
its icy suffocations.

PETIT DEJEUNER

I sing a song
of the croissant
and of the wily French
who trick themselves daily
back to the world
for its sweet ceremony.
Ah to be reeled
up into morning
on that crisp,
buttery
hook.

THIS UNCOMMON BANANA

Curved,
yellower
than a sickle moon
it tops the cornucopia
of unbruised fruit,
in a nimbus of candlelight.

Not the smiling hostess
nor the serving man
in Sunday pants
will ever notice
that I've taken it
away.

neckbones n sauerkraut

twenty-two nutmeg arms
reach for the pot

pass the pot
clockwise

first daddy's
big bass hands
then
round the table
down to
me

one lone neckbone
a few strands of
kraut

pass the
hot sauce

suck the last bone
suck the milk from
the last bone
suck the last love bone
down like
momma's
breast

BLACKBERRY JUBILEE

"Give me the big ones,"
Granddaddy used to say,
squeezing Grandma's hand—
"not those little nothing nubbins
with no room to sink your teeth,
but the kind that keeps sticking
in the cracks of back molars—
the kind you have to dig out
with your tongue—
the kind that's hung around
just long enough it drops
into your hand, faintly
fermenting, drives the bees wild."

THE PLUM

Dark globe that fits easily into the palm,
your skin is speckled with pale galaxies,
an endless scattering.
Everywhere Adam and Eve are leaving
the Garden. You are the fruit we pluck
and eat. We need no serpent to urge us,
drawn as we are to your swelling,
your purple shading to rose, your skin
that yields to the touch, to the teeth:
all the world's waters and all its sweetness
rolled into fruit that explodes
on the tongue. We eat and drink flesh
the color of garnets, rubies, wounds.
It is bitter just under the skin.

MY MOTHER WANTS LAMB CHOPS, STEAKS, LOBSTER, ROAST BEEF

Something to get
her teeth in.
Forget the shakes
cancer patients
are supposed to
choose, forget
tapioca pudding,
vanilla ice
she wants what
is full of blood,
something to
chew, to get
the red color
out of, something
she can attack
fiercely. My
mother who never
was namby pamby,
never held her
tongue, never
didn't attack
or answer back,
worry about
angering or hurt-
ing anybody but
said what she
felt and wouldn't
walk any tight

rope, refuses the
pale and delicate
for what's blood,
what she can
chew, even spit
out if she
needs to

EASY

While she starts the water and measures the pasta,
he sets the table and peels the garlic,
she cuts up broccoli, strips snow peas, readies fish,
he presses the garlic, fixes her a kir, him a gin,
she sautes the vegetables while he grates cheese,
fixes the candles, puts flowers on the table,
she puts pasta in the boiling water, fixes salad,
which he takes to the table with the cheese,
she mixes a salad dressing by hand, he opens the wine
and takes it to the table where everything is ready,
except for the pasta, so he lights the candles
and puts salad from a big walnut bowl into small ones.

Now she or he brings the pasta, greens and fish
mixed in, and they sit to talk, drink wine and eat.
Though October, they sit on a small screen porch
in the back of the house where they have lived
for twelve years of their twenty together,
the last six, the children gone, alone.
Once, during dinner, if they stop talking
and listen to the music, they will, without drama,
hold hands a moment, almost like a handshake
by now, most friendly, confirming the contract,
and more. She is a pretty woman of 51, who has
kept trim and fit. He is 56 and hasn't.

Later, they will clear the dishes and clean up,
and she will bring tea and fresh fruit to bed,
where they will watch a little television or not,
with herbal tea and the fruit. After that, if
they make love or not, they will talk a long time,
her work or his, the budget, the middle east,
this child or that, how good dinner was, how
easy it is, the times like this, when it's simple.

FOR YOU AT YOUR PARENTS' HOUSE

*For Sedgwick Heskett in
St. Paul, Minnesota*

Today I thought of you.
This morning, awake between sleeps, I thought,
"gossamer wings, tiny strong strings
connect me to you."
(I could pull you back as necessary.)

At the market, I bought only foods in season and
organic—timely and unpolluted, appropriate and
safe.

I prepared turnips.
I had always hated turnips, bitter and hard,
rough, scarred fruit of my parents' making. But
today
the turnips were huge and succulent, purple-white
breasts, middle-aged ones at that,
of a woman lying down, nipples tiny and nubbly,
long, fresh, lush leaves growing green into her
body.

We ate the leaves too, bright sparkles in our
creamy, creamy soup,
plump turnip bits that swam like scallops in a
happy sea.

I thought of you as I julienned the beets.
More roots, of blood this time, just as
thick as water, not more.
By this time, you too were thinking of food. It
was dinnertime in St. Paul.

I had called and gotten your father's phone number
just in case, imagining what I would tell your
parents to get you on the phone: "Her cat's had
kittens." "Just wanted her to know her house was
all right." "Just thought I'd say 'hi.'" Hm.

I slipped their skins off, rough, dark scarlet.
And delivered their shiny babies' heads,
round and smooth and new.
Never seen before.

THE TREE HOUSE

Have you seen our mulberry tree
And the neighborhood children
With purple lips and blue fingers
Climbing to the house
In its branches?

LUNCHBOX

P-U it stinks in here cried the bottle of delicate cologne
as loudly as she could P-U P-U

the liverwurst turned over inside the sheets of his sandwich
& went back to sleep

a red-skinned apple tried to pretend he didn't know her language
& anyway he was nearly impermeable

the can of Coca-Cola might as well have been dead he was so
little help so close to catatonic

the priestly dental floss smiled benignly & rubbed his thin
hands together inside his cassock confident that in the end
the lady's plight wouldn't be so bad

in their box the raisins belched & farted on each other
but so gently no one noticed

ignoring them all, completely at peace inside the lid, a
decal of Daisy Mae fishing, bamboo pole between her toes,
stalk of grass in her teeth, in the sunny Appalachian hills

& at work he recalls what
he's gotten his girlfriend for when they meet at noon

EATING SNOW

He picks up the snow when the day has been warm.
He turns it, feels its weight, then attacks cold
with his teeth till they ache, and then he hears
thick ice melting all around him. He eats and sees
the creeks splash faster, hears gaunt trees whisper
on the golf course below while they grope blindly
like prisoners in a condemned cell to dying light.

His tv talks tirelessly about this season of hope,
but the chemistry professor on the news has doubts,
warns him of the snow he scoops in ungloved hands,
speaks of lead and death from the Sony at his feet.
He goes out to the sunset to straighten things out.
He bends down, scoops up some snow, and puts it in
his mouth, to taste again the day that's been warm.

FOOD

Word hangs like eyes peering
between two ears. No chance to

grow up to be anybody. Two O's
and a couple of consonants

couldn't possibly be something
we can't live without. Still

that's what hangs there, the start
of foolish with Orphan Annie eyes.

Tastes like your foot's asleep,
he said, talking of fake chocolate.

And Annie Dillard dared to say
the preying mantis ate the hummingbird,

it was food. Anything is food if
you eat it, isn't it? In last night's

dream I hustled my friends away from
the party after I learned the hostess

planned to eat us. Hostess cupcakes.
Did I go to bed hungry? Don't I always?

WATER

Thirst is the worst hunger
you will ever know
Only water quenches it
not Pepsi or even beer—
just water. City water
with its beer head will do.

Thirst creeps to the water
hole, moistens finger tips,
remembers melting ice
on childhood's ethered tongue—
desert lust, palate's longing.
Thirst is the worst hunger.

CARCASS

Eat it
Eat the chicken carcass
now,
or I'll make it walk down your
throat,
bones and all.

That's what he said to me
on April 23rd at 7 p.m.

And I
I was stupid enough to cut a
piece
and choke it down
to prove my
love.

WISDOM POEM

Chew slowly
not only for the taste,
but for the rich noise
of that great mill of your maw
and for the brazen flexing
of those muscled hinges.
Eating is all of this,
and more.

It is waiting
a long time
between swallows.

Feel those twinned harrows
arc apart, meet, rub,
release, and meet again—
one glad curve partly
enclosing the other.

And your tongue,
that old dodger,
let it have its head,
sliding and swirling about
like Peggy Fleming,
or cleaning the blades,
shoveling,
sore with delight.

Eating is all of this
and more.

APPETITES

Because yesterday I ate shark steak,
the thunder walks for hours on the house,
the boneless hips of giant fish snake
toward the town. Because the filets, scored
from the dorsal side, wavered in the frying pan
like flung birds, the Bradford Pear bows down
to its knobbed knees to give full lift and sway
to wingless things whose silhouettes darken
the stark sky under which I have to navigate.
Because the meat of the shark tasted as clean
as chicken would if chickens had the chance
to eat the sea, the black in this place swallows
the light that I have made to hide myself away.
Tomorrow, because the shark has lost all of his skin
and his only blood vein, I must offer my legs
to the sea, up to my belly in fingers and feathers
of surf. I have other mouths to feed because
yesterday I ate a sound I never had the chance
to hear, nor wanted to, nor knew I did, till now.

THE FLOWER CART AND THE BUTCHER

Today in le Marché Saint-Germain I hear
two widows, stuffed into their coats
like flour in two patched sacks, and the one
grousing in the bloodied light off a strung-up boar
—all bristle and hulled gut and clear crazed eye—,
and the one, who is getting the plump of a partridge,
tells her twin

      "If you remember three generations
of war it is enough, you remember your father
who ate spaniel under the Siege, your husband
who was dismembered in '17,
and your brother who was a prisoner in Suisse
and it cost a good deal of money . . ."

      "Pah," says the other

—and there behind them
(where the left-handed butcher Claude, who has the touch,
had made an arrangement) three cock-pheasants
like blades of the court in a travesty of flight
and a poor petit-gris, without even a coat
for the season, tied up by the neck
and cutting his caper on nothing—

      "Pah," says sister mole,

"always the same:
the men plow and plant
but the women will do the harvesting."

      . . .

      "Yes," I said,
easing a way between, for there

was a boy I knew, a meatpacker
down from les Halles,

        "yes, but will you look at
the slaver of bull on beauty's shoulder!
It eclipses, Ladies;
      the tropic in the citrus,
        it takes the Octoberish
moon out of the pumpkin,
      and it makes full melons blanch! By the beard
        on a woman last seen at the Denkman Circus
and by all the neglected saints, I swear
it will scab the blush on that pushcart of dyed carnations!"

Well the two of them stupidly stood there,
like a matched pair of Guernseys appalled by a wattled Brahman,
and would not budge,

      "Yes!" I insisted, for Tony
(and that was his name) was stepping
now into the street
and turning a white smock toward la rue des Quatre Vents.

      "*Yes!* (and I may have been shrilling)
Oh merciful YES—and you'll be pleased to shovel
a thumb into a dumpling!
      Envisagez,
mes vieilles tantines, the shattered crystal,

    Le Fouquet's et La Tour d'Argent, Maxim's
    all sharded in soup tureens
    —Sister in Heaven! Imaginez—
    —*essayez de vous faire une idée*—
    the ill-shaved hysterical chefs
    disguising crow and tuber, mice
    and odder things caught crawling in a root cellar . . ."

—*"Here!* Give me that flayed squirrel!"
I shouted at Claude.

              So I took its pinkish pale flesh,
all swaddled in butchers' crepe and studded
like something rare with a heart
and two uncut, incarnadine kidneys.
And I muttered a lullaby and hushed it a dirge
as I crossed la rue Lobineau and la rue Mabillon.
I came down the smoked flank of the church
and crossed myself twice, singing
in a cracked tenor "Dieu de misère! O Dieu de misère!"
Then I commanded a coup de rouge, and here
(if nobody's noticed)
is where me and the mascot still are.

The speaker is "Doc' Dan Mahoney," the model for Djuna Barnes's
celebrated "Dr. Matthew-Mighty-grain-of-salt-Dante O'Connor," in her
novel *Nightwood.* The poem is spoken in Paris in the fall of 1939, during
"the phony war" which preceded the defeat of France and the Nazi
occupation. Anyone trying to imagine a beseiged Paris at that time would
have thought back to the two sieges in 1870 and 1871, when first the
Prussians isolated and starved the city and then the French isolated and
starved The Paris Commune. Accounts of that induced famine—and the
ingenuity with which it was met—are astonishing.

"The Flower Cart and the Butcher" was inspired in part by Jean Hélion's
painting *La voiture de fleurs et le boucher* (1964): in the center bright
scarlet flowers—carnations?—cascade from the cart toward the viewer; to
the left an elderly person (perhaps a blind man) passes behind the cart and
to the right the merchant wraps a bouquet in white paper. To the right of
the merchant and behind him, about the pass behind the cart at the same
moment as the old man, "un fort de la Halle" or "meat-packer" carries a
huge side of beef, also brilliant red, that rises up over the hood of his
white smock, drapes down his shoulder and back, and seems to flare like a
wind-blown cape.

DOMESTIC

When he told his houseboy he'd
had enough of this Moroccan shit,
that he wanted to start seeing some
good French cuisine, or his ass was grass,
the cook said nothing.

The next hors d'oeuvres was baby eel,
like sperm, in boiling garlic oil and
the entree involved three little brains
swimming in tomato paste. By that time
all the restaurants had closed.

All we
know of
love

LOLLYGAGGING

So this is how we'll hold back death for now:
Some apricots and chocolate; Cummings, unread;
And ripened plums, that renewed a thickening bough,

In a wooden bowl beside the open window.
This elemental warmth, the marriage bed—
This is how we'll hold back death for now.

Your limbs that pull me closer show me how
An August day meanders past all dread;
Such ripened plums renew the thickening bough.

And as my wayward finger runs your brow
You drift, as if we'll never join the dead;
This is how we hold back death for now.

The throb of bodies, the liberty of vow,
The weld of touch, and fortune left unsaid—
These ripened plums renew the thickening bough.

Deliberate love, the shine of *I* and *Thou*:
Let love enfold us till all the heat has fled.
This is how we hold back death, for now;
The ripened plums renew the thickest bough.

PEARS

Some say
it was a pear
Eve ate.
Why else the shape
of the womb,
or of the cello
whose single song is grief
for the parent tree?
Why else the fruit itself
tawny and sweet
which your lover
over breakfast
lets go your pear-
shaped breast
to reach for?

ATTEMPTING MAGIC

for Susan Valenza

You and I aspire to estuaries.

Take a breath and come home early
with scallops from Linoleum, Maryland.

The wine we chill has a life
in its light behind the door.

Tonight our improvisation is
hipbone to thigh at countertop.

This bowl retains the memory
of flowers born of lichen.

Admiring such tenacity
over steaming plates of presto,

I am yours.

DICKINSON IN WINTER

Little by little, she withdrew,
preferring frost, the empty
chalice where sun couldn't reach,
the way love, reckless,

had reached and entered, grown
so large it threatened to crack her,
the way the doorknocker's thunder
cracked through rooms locked in ice.

Irises in their vases,
silent, voluptuous as revolvers,
shuddered and clicked shut. The wind
swept past them up the stairs.

Look at the stained door
where her form once stood,
a tree struck by lightning.
Raise your arm like a branch

recalling its scorched gift. Here
is her presence, then, fragrant
bitter as incense
against the icy backdrop of thought.

TAROT CARD IV. EMPEROR

It was you I should have married.
That was our trouble all along,
the source of disappointment.
Here I thought it was
my too red lipstick,
my turnIng away.

I never gave you credit
and want to do it now.
You were the one who took
me to the doctor, paid my bills,
even cooked my food.
Although we rarely spoke,
you drove me to my school.

I realize now that every promise,
possible and impossible,
is all we know of love.
I didn't understand you
and took myself away
but a person abandoned
waits for eternity.

I see you everywhere I go
in doorways—
driving that far car.
If I marry you now
the failures that curdled the milk
in our kitchen
could be set right.
I could cook Christmas dinner
making it lovely with berries
and the devotion of a daughter.

Baleful ceremonies forgot, I
would spend my last dime
on flowers for your table,
the solid water of childhood
melting a new flow,
breaking a morning with the gods,
a new snow,
our melancholy faces gone
along with anger
behind the curtains drawn
between us.

The stones we swallowed multiplied
until we could hardly walk
and now are cooked away
beside the festive table.
Although the world is emptied
of one more person,
we float toward each other
and this is the way
the past is forgiven.

In this cathedral
we could still marry.
It's not too late,
if you will take me as I take you,
as we did not take each other then. I do.

FULL MOON ON K STREET

The moon has your face tonight,
hiding behind black-violet veils
of clouds, coy, intimating nothing.

Like an orange outside the grasp
of a starving child, you stab my heart.
All longing is the same.

No natural light penetrates
this street; the lampposts rule.
The high-rises have mothered

them from their concrete wombs,
bidding us rejoice in coldness,
disdaining the celestial tease.

The moon has phases. Though I pray
not, you might be one. The clouds
pull tight, tight around your mouth.

FITTING

Bridesmaids, the five of us stand
in our slips, all ages and shapes showing,
waiting for her to drape the red silk,
let out the hips, take in
the cowl neck. The folds at the waist
will hide that tummy bulge, she whispers
from between her pins and lips.
Quietly bridled, we give ourselves
to her practiced eye, then shed the new chance
of each perfected dress.

In the closet, my wedding dress yellows.
This anniversary, one rose stood
for a dozen. Aspirin in the vase, and still
the bud stayed closed. I expected twice the life—
a week later buried it, shriveled and black,
under supper's chicken bones.

The calendar moves toward fall,
I stand in the rose-colored dress.
During the vows I hold my bouquet,
all shades of red, next to the bride's white orchids—
hand hers back after the bridegroom's kiss.
My tears don't come until you lay
your arm across me in the dark—
I'm singing and sewing my own white dress,
each day like crystal. It fits again,
and we dance, your spice-smell a meadow
with two young horses—far away.
The dress slips off, the music rises
like the smell of earth plowed for winter,
the tang of apples and sweet herbs,
the colts becoming one colt prancing.

BANQUET

to Katherine

Bones laid bare to teeth
again, flesh hard-salted

to small, unswallowed wishes
        for sons & one more daughter;

the wishbone, wine-soaked, broken now
            you holding one, I the other.

A coffee filter. The spill
of table linen, and guests gone home

to fold themselves
to bed & useless prayer.

Their empty dishes up
            at you, can only stare

as for hours, after the dinner watch
        we ladle the sweet sauce of looks
& talk across ripe, uneaten pear.

How the candled body sings:
Feast & appetite
feast & appetite

what, but the love of bones
ever set our table right?

SENTIMENT: noise

Take a stretch across this bared breast. A physical
motion to release snap. You shut. Cut up paper rock.
A desire you should have remembered but never. Wasn't there.
T.V. ad. Glowing gems forgot the water. Trust this.
It is sunrise in your arms. We walk on your cool forested beach.
I take you mountain walking. You fix me breakfast bed.
I buy you fireplace flower gifts. You call me secret names. I forget
other other's and accompanying want. You tell your friends.
I speak secret words. You tell magic charms. I speak louder
shouts. You invoke dark witches. I scream. You spell.
I don't understand. You do. Stop.

We walk by fresh laundry smells. Lunch time milk money.
This safe room sometimes scary at night. The sounds come in.
Our legacy places are empty full. We speak the stuffing out.
More volume to quiet down. Reach around. Take.
This hand, out. Bleeding too.

I'M IN LOVE WITH THE MORTON SALT GIRL

I'm in love with the Morton salt girl.
I want to pour salt in her hair and watch
her dance. I want to walk with her through the
salt rain and pretend that it is water. I want to
get lost in the Washington Cathedral and follow her
salt trail to freedom.

I want to discover her salt lick in the forests of Virginia.
I want to stand in line for hours to see her walk on in
the middle of a movie only to have the film break and watch salt
pour out and flood the aisles. I want to sit in an empty theater
up to my eyeballs in salt and dream of her.

When I go home she will be waiting for me in her white dress
and I will drink salt water and lose my bad dreams.
I will seek the blindness of salt, salt down my wounds,
hang like a side of ham over the curtain rod in the bathroom
and let her pour salt directly on my body.

When she is done I will lick her salty lips with my tongue
and walk her down the stairs into the rain wishing that I
could grow gills and bathe in her vast salt seas.

THREE SONGS

after Solomon

I.

He wants you to save his life.
To raise pillars of silver
Under his billowing silken tent.
Eyes of doves, belly of bright ivory.

Go up to the palm tree
Take hold of its boughs
And bring his desire toward you.

You ravish his heart
With the scent of your garments.
The flock lies down at noon.
Shadows flee. The king is held.

Now, given all the substance
Of his house, your vineyard,
Which is yours, you must give to him.

Come early to the gates: you will find
The locks open with the drops of the night
Upon an orchard of pomegranates.
Make haste with your love.

II.

Dove's eyes, our bed is green.
The rafters of our house are strong.
My shadow held in your shadow
Dances upon sweet-scented walls.

This is our banqueting house.
The winter is past; all winters
Pass into spring, inevitably.
Behold this purple valley, how

I become the Rose of Sharon,
Grown in the clefts of the rock
Where your voice breaks the day,
A pillar of smoke—no, of silver.

III.

Until the spring is shut,
The fountain sealed, these
Vines will never cease to bear.

This is the feast of our days,
A heap of wheat set with lilies,
Honey and myrrh, milk and tender grapes.

In the palace of silver and cedar,
The vineyard of a thousand,
In the king's orchard, the shadow of the palm,

All manner of pleasant fruits,
New and old, I have been storing for you.
Make haste with your love.

CHRYSOBERYL

Deep within the cat's eye
my love winks at me.
Sly and lascivious
a true coupling of eyelids.
Unexpected. Like the time
he pinched my bottom at a party
when I was passing the potatoes.

Honey I say blowing off the dust
from dead filing cabinets ragged
cardboard boxes. What you doin'
down there? You're supposed to be
in Idaho six feet under.

Another wink equally distracting.
I spit upon the eye
polish it on the short hairs
rub the stone between my palms.
Blood-stains smear the surface
tasting of ambrosia when I lick them off.

My palms still bleed at vacant intervals.
What do I do now?
Father I've acquired the stigmata,
Shall I wear a hair shirt?
Do twenty lashes?
Am I a saint?

Do not disturb yourself, my daughter.
Go home and take a cooling shower
with all your clothes on.
Such hallucinations often trouble
women of your age.

hungry eyes

you say you're starved,
i give you a feast of
kisses simmered in warm wetness
you say you're famished
i give you a banquet of
finger tips marinated in hot caresses
you say you're hungry,
i give you a supper of
passion garnished by moist movements

at dawn's light
we lay twisted
like ebony bones
upon a festival table
last night's passion still
warm in our filled hearts
i stroke your face
as your eyes reveal
a new hunger waiting
to be fed.

LOVE STORY

When the most charming man in Bulgaria
Has butchered, cooked and fed his pig
Nadia to thirty close friends—Nadia,
Whom he adored but could no longer

Keep in the grains to which she had
Become accustomed—you know things
In the new socio-capitalist economy
Are too hard: beautiful two hundred

Fifty pounds of bristle-white, 10-inch
Snout, hungry, offended, and amorously
Squealing her lover Plamen to fetch
The slops and corn of his troth.

Bless Plamen and forgive him, Lord,
Who tried to be a good pig-priest:
With friends to pour the blood and wine,
To burn God's portion, pray and baste.

Flesh
stirred
to a
touch

POEM

The swans on the river, a great
flotilla in the afternoon sun
in October again.

In a fantasy, Yeats saw himself appear
to Maud Gonne as a swan,
his plumage fanning his desire.

One October at Coole Park
he counted fifty-nine wild swans.
He flushed them into a legend.

Lover by lover is how he said they flew,
but one of them must have been without a mate.
Why did he not observe that?

We talk about Zeus and Leda and Yeats
as if they were real people, we identify constellations
as if they were drawn there on the night.

Cygnus and Castor & Pollux
are only ways of looking at
scatterings of starry matter,

a god putting on swan-flesh
to enter a mortal girl
is only a way of looking at love-trouble.

The violence and calm of these big fowl!
When I am not with you
I am always the fifty-ninth.

SHE REMEMBERS THE FIRST TIME

He took her hand and drew it down
to a heat-nest of hair, to a column
base—her belly recoiled—but her hand,
obedient, lightly tried the surface,
smooth it was, resilient, alive.

Once in Mr. Haskell's boat an eel
had spiralled up her arm, a green coil
thick as rope and slick, the muscle of it
pressing her muscle—its small sloped eye
malevolent. Where was this fear born?

Back in viney dreams of fruit-heavy branches
where something stirred troubling the leaves,
in an image of thick fingers on a window-ledge,
her leap across the dark cave beneath the bed,
and taunt of boys practicing strut and swagger.

Later, when melon sweetness laced the air,
desire ripened and her flesh, taut with summer,
stirred to a touch, a sudden loosening, layers
falling away as pleasure slid over the ledge
of fear and she gave her body to astonishment.

THE NAMELESS

By age twenty I had lost count of them.
　　　　There were too many men
　　　　　　　　I let float through my sheets,
the ones who wanted to float
　　　　　　　and those who tried to pull me down.
　　　　　　　　But I would not be anchored,
leaving behind a trail of men,
the flotsam and jetsam of the human heart.

If there was a moon back then
　　　　　　　I can't recall it.
　　　　　　　　If there were stars, they were pinpoints
punctuating a larger blackness.
　　　　　　I thought nothing could touch me,
　　　　　　　　got more convinced the more
men I let touch my skin.

I specialized in guitarists.
　　　　　　I liked the coke sneaked backstage
　　　　　　　　and hanging out in darkened bars.
There was a drummer with a German girlfriend
　　　　　　who he taught only one phrase in English.
　　　　　　　　She'd recite it in halting tones
to any man who approached the table:
　　　　　　Fuck off, peckerhead. I liked to hear her say it,
　　　　　　　　liked to get the peckerhead to buy us drinks
and join us anyway, while my guitarist
　　　　　　glared from the stage.
　　　　　　　　Peckerhead, guitarist: two more nameless souls
advancing across my bed.
　　　　　　One true word from either and I was off
　　　　　　　　to the next in a long firing line of strangers.
For isn't that all the future holds,

whether you fuck them or not?
        I averted my eyes from the richest food,
as only the terminally hungry can.
        I let my hunger define me,
            although, like so many men,
I didn't even know its name.

FIRST FLAME

The heart engages before
the brain's extrapolation
can say why. He was new,
a boy who could play
clarinet *and* piano, as smart
as anyone in our school where tracts
were set from birth and ranks
were seldom broken.

He laughed a lot, hoarse
I might have said, but say
like a raucous wind roaring
through the junipers of our street.
And he was skinny before "gaunt"
could be romantic to remember.
I had no words, nor needed any;
the brain busied itself with sound,

and the image of him riding his privileged
blue bicycle late into dusk, into the pungent
smoke that rose from rusted trash drums
tilting on edges of alleys all over fifties Kansas.
And out of the busyness that puts "first"
with "best" and makes "desire," how clearly
the brain speaks, how clearly it remembers
the whole song when night hums these few bars:

when the first star twirled like a baton
blazing in the sun's retreat, pulling down
the backdrop for the troupe to shine
against, we two lined up our eyes
on that wishing point, divided heaven
into halves and began counting.
And in my yard where planets hung thickest,
sooner or later he fell with me into the sky.

NEW IN CARTONS

Tuesday, I want you
with every breath
of wind that stirs;
all my raging parts
and indelicate
howl your name
in unison.

Wednesday,
I chew up the idea
of you and spew
bones, feathers, scales, fur.
I don't need you.
I don't get it.

Friday,
I wouldn't know you
if you rang the doorbell
and tried to sell me
a vacuum cleaner
new in cartons.

last nite

last nite
as I eased into sleep
a midnite horn eased into me.

last nite
a saxophone's lonesome moan
nestled between my sheets.
It made me wail
—this was no safe sax—
its voice traveled thigh-high
through my hi fi.
together we cried
    ooh, baby
    yes, lawd
    hallelujah
    get down.

last nite
that sax taught me
carnal knowledge and high praises.
it made me say my bedtime prayers
in a musical tongue.
we had church on a king-sized bed.

last nite
the saxophone made love to me.
the saxophone made me ready for love.
ready
to mate my spirituality with my sexuality
ready
to leap tall men in a single bound
ready
to get filled with the most holy

last nite
a saxophone made me ready for love
tonite and now,
are you ready for me?

A MATTER OF CHOICE

"Pet or meat?" the braless
woman asks. Under each arm
she cradles a rabbit. This

is a woman who knows how
to kill: "Just lay them
on the ground and lop off

their heads." And how
to give pleasure—her two
thumbs press a vein in each

rabbit's neck. Love,
sometimes when you enter
I bare my teeth. Salt

or sweet? The body decides
since the body must answer
to curious, various hungers.

CATHEDRAL

It is a perfect day to remember your belly,
the religious facade of your shimmering white
surrender on the sidewalk in front of the deli
on R Street, where I held you tight.

You used to sit at a little table, a pink
book about Picasso in your lap, a doctrinaire
look in your eye. I bought you a drink
and later took you to my lair.

The exchange was extraordinarily complex.
Brutal myths became so colorfully private.
Your lips, your lips, your lips—I took sex
from everything you looked at, everything you ate.

Then those small, pink Picassos caught up with us.
A new air, a new light gave us a sense
of perfection. I began to notice how the focus
blurred, how lyrical was my embrace of absence.

INVITATION TO THE DANCE

I'll be in disguise, wearing
skin stretched so drumtight over my bones
that you won't know me. You'll look
in vain for me (softbellied, ripe) across the room
but I will dance clear-eyed and brazen
up to you so rogue bold in my disguise
that you won't guess me. My eyes will invite you
into the havoc of my heart,
and you will feel the shudder of recognition
as I take your measure. Just penetrate
this wacked out disguise / romp bawdy with me
through one whirling night. Then we will stand tight,
tight together, like the stones of the Pyramids. No mortar,
yet you can't slip a knife in between.

AUNT FROM THE COUNTRY

The wedding was perfect—heirloom
dress, the groom somber with joy.
Later, an aunt from the country grew
bawdy and danced with a waiter until
the band packed up.

                She'd driven home
singing to herself, recalling music,
her body's sway, young men leaping,
lofting a blue garter. His hand
had been hard, sweaty, and he'd
held her eyes even as young girls
twisted round them.

                She remembered
ceremony and the falling away of ceremony,
how, without gloves, she'd felt flesh,
and for a moment hunger hollowed
her body like the suck before
a wave that drains mudflats,
exposes a hull slick with weed,
a shimmer of fish flailing the surface.

On the porch next day she smelled
dry rot she'd not noticed before,
like a barn abandoned or hay left
too long unturned and with a J-bar
she pulled the weathered plank,
it lifted with a cry, carrying
rosettes of puncture wounds.

She planed a fresh board, its grain
pink, surface smooth, the corners

she squared, and her hammer hit clean
as nails took the wood, the last tap
neat as the click of a goat's hoof.

Arms crossed, she stood hugging
herself. The plank gleamed, wind
sharpened carrying the smell of salt.
It was a fine wedding, good to dance,
good, the waiter's small curved smile.

BULLS

The farmer down the road put two
Black Angus bulls into my pasture
Where they were in residence for a month.
Big as freight cars, shoulders bursting
With black ballocks the size of soccer balls
And complex pouches hanging underneath
From which a pizzle red as a torch
Forayed from time to time, they vacuumed up
The grass and sometimes tried to hump each other
But gave up quickly. They were indifferent
To my presence: they waited for but one thing
And I was not it.
They were taken off one afternoon
And in their place nine Black Angus cows
Came to stay, some ready for love.
They wandered about, splattered with their own flop,
Wearing clouds of flies, sprouting orange
Tags from each ear and wheeling
Like a flock of birds as I walked in their field.
I did not think they were particularly
Attractive. And yet I know those bulls would kill
To be where I was—
Those black haunches! That Paradise!

HUNGER

Southern Africa. Gaborone, Botswana.
Two whites at a table.

In the bar nobody's smoking
but him, and the girl he's next to
is obviously uncomfortable, liking him,
but unable to stand the fumes. Finally
she goes ahead, waves them from her face:
he seems not to notice,
keeps on puffing,
until, a cigarette later, she does it again,
and then again,
so that some sort of a look comes into his eyes
and he grinds it out: gently, compassionately,
like a life.

He keeps on talking, yes, he wants her,
she wants him—and I watch
as, in conversation, her mouth
forms the word: *Jaanong?* (Well?)
And he sits there, glancing from the girl
to the cigarettes, weighing,
valuing, balancing: perfectly trapped,
like some wild animal
halfway between the headlights.

APOSTROPHE

O Goddess of Opportunity!
you called to me unexpectedly
years ago in a Maryland bank lobby.
My hand had the stairwell door
to return from an escrow deposit
when I heard "Howard" shouted
with female joy. Turned round
overwhelmed by the tousle of blond
California hair, warmth of tanned
California torso, invite of wide
California hips half-hidden inside
sunny shorts, amber arms and bold
California legs placed just so
one before the other, yellow cotton
halter blouse tied loosely between
California breasts above which
nestled a captivating come-
hither California smile. I
did not recognize you from high school.
You seemed to have emerged newborn
and dry from the Pacific, raising
unpeaceful passions in me. I,
dressed as a three-piece lawyer,
was not prepared, reacted
like a cartoon character: smoke
whistled from my nose and ears,
a fire alarm clanged in my head,
my tongue came out, grew
in amazement, as did my popped
eyes. I flashed through hot colors
to red, sizzled to ash before you.
Your smile broadened slightly

and nestled more deeply in your breasts.
I remember saying you looked great
and wanting to drop the deposit slip,
forget that old farmer upstairs,
my client, awestruck by shelves of
leather-bound law, wanting to run off
with you anywhere, somewhere,
nowhere, to a room without windows,
without a door, but alas!
the inertia of marriage and job. We
settled for histories: you back
visiting from California, me hiding
the left hand.
Now you return to me—
divorced from the wife
and the law, bifocaled, teeth
crowned, paunchy and balding—
in dream. O Ghost of Lost
Opportunity, we run off!
and I wake shaking, haunted
by where in my head
you have hidden so long.

The perfect room

is curved, a shell streaked
with the colors of dawn and earth.
As you lie beside me, your shoulder
is a hill in moonlight.
I taste your salt.
The walls, bone-strong
around us, grow to fit
the live animal at the center.

When that animal is hungry, her foot
moves in waves, envelops her prey,
and forces its valves open
so she can feed on the soft parts.

You dream our house
is flooded. I imagine waves,
grey tipped with white, rushing
through our rooms. Gulls circle,
crying their raucous need,
waiting for the dead fish to rise.

I used to bury whelks in the sand.
Days later, I'd dig up the shell,
clean and empty, the mollusk gone.

In her foot, the living conch
forms capsules to seal her eggs in.
She binds them to a dead shell or stone,
a train of cradles rocked by the ocean
until they burst, spilling babies
to the waves.

Let the ocean rock us,
return us to that room
of dawn and earth and skin.
Let the shell grow from within,
large enough to shelter
the dark animal.

AT THE SEDONA CAFE

She contains herself, drawing him in,
But she wants to kneel and kiss
the ground he stands on, the man
in blue jeans, sexy, bending
over the espresso machine.
To run her hands over him.

She can almost taste his ribs,
those raw wristbones,
the hollow place at his throat
just deep enough for her
finger to flower in. She can
see in the dark she's so wise.

She flutters and drops her eyes
to his belt. In her heart
already she has cast him in pure
gold. He has no name yet.
She watches him reach
for the shining cup and fill it.

THE CRUSH

At this mellow age (and me a feminist)
how can I squander twenty minutes
matching ear hoops to my saffron vest?
I could say I've found Jung's soulful animus.
I could drag in Father Freud and wisely sigh.
I could sublimate my middle years in Spring
and mention nymphs. He's *young* (twenty-two
or -three). It's ridiculous—and I'm a fool.
There are poems to write and death and taxes,
braces for the girls, the rising cost of milk.
I must seize my garden's lush, rambunctious
weeds and spay the cat.

                              Yet he is lovely,
solemn, and very tall and has this way
of peering through his glasses, waiting
for life to hit him broadside,
I suppose. He wants to be prepared.
His russet mane tangles to his shoulders.
He wears these funky boots and shyly jokes.
I stroll to the library where he works
and snatch some random books on French, films,
finbacks, farce. We chat. He yearns for Yeats'
golden, singing bird; I like Roethke's goose.

Nothing will ever happen. That's a loss,
I guess, but makes the whole thing more delicious:
those green eyes, the warm hairs at his wrist.
My imagination revs its hormones
'til I want to grab his Georgetown shirt
and shout, "Good luck! Enjoy," as if he's starting
on a journey and I'm a long way off,
passing on a different ship and waving,
throwing kisses with both hands. *Mi amour!*

Mi ami! Je t'aime, Je t'aime! I want to toss
confetti in his Botticelli hair,
polish off a dozen champagne toasts,
dance in red shoes to some Caribbean tunes.
I want to hang over the stern
and holler through a brutal wind:
"Ain't life a raucous bitch!"—
even as the indifferent ocean
muscles in, and our separate vessels slip
into the ceaseless waves
of bric-a-brac and grief.

         I hand him my card;
he stamps my seven books; we say good-bye.
On the way home, my earrings release
their tiny sparkles, I buy four lamb chops
at the market, and when my husband asks
about my day, I say, "Oh, it was nice."

EPITHET

The first man I called Sir
the wrong way, not meaning it, was the one
who stopped his black Chevy on the hill
near high school, Could I come over
& show him the route to West
Cherry Lane? I could, he didn't
look dirty or strange, just grown-up
but young, with a dark plaid shirt
& his sleeves turned up, & a road map
unfolded over the steering,
like my father, on trips. I was trying
to see where he pointed, when I couldn't
help seeing his other hand hefting
something below, it looked
alive but somehow skinned over,
like sausage. I knew he wanted
me to think it was really all him.
He wasn't ugly or anything
different, he had a regular nose,
his eyes were dark & real serious,
giving orders somehow. He was handsome
in fact. This was all broad daylight,
& houses I knew, my regular
route. So I called him Sir
& more Sir, pretending I thought
nothing was wrong, while I backed
away from his arm, which had hairs
like the minister's, & the closed car door,
& got back to the papers I'd been folding
on the storm drain corner. His car
drove off up the hill, getting smaller,

like a little black toy. The street
stayed empty. I looked down at my jeans,
which were brand-new from Penney's, with a plaid,
red-&-white, lining the cuffs.

Next day, in the lunchroom, I started
to tell my best friends, at the end
of the table. They giggled a lot,
Was he handsome? Did he ask you to hold it?
Did he show you his money? I wanted
to ask was it really all him,
but didn't know how. Then Agnes,
who was bigger, said he was just a pervert,
they always came out in the spring
back home, why once, there was one waiting
at the bus stop, with his fly wide open,
& she & her cousins just laughed
& pointed, till he cussed them out
& ran off in the woods. Just a pervert,
that's all. I felt better, & thirsty
& hungry. Agnes had finished
most of my lunch, which was chowder
with franks, so she gave me her pie,
which was cinnamon apple with topping,
& better than usual. So I had
two desserts, before the bell rang.

PLEASE

enough
already
said the key
to the lock   i know
i scratched you   scar tissue
closing you off but that was
never my intention   things
sometimes get out of hand
take a direction you
can never anticipate
when cornered with a
yes no maybe not
allowed i'm
reduced to lies
not meant to
hurt but to
protect you
let me ease
down into
the dark
curves
i know by
heart
i can
make you
come
around
for
me

NICE

it's nice to have
a beer
in the middle of the afternoon
say about 3:30
as if you had nothing
better
to do   nothing
to lose
thinking about all
those poor stiffs working
the loading dock who'll be
too beat after years
of it
to get stiff anymore
until they're laid out   stiff
a phony peace painted
on their mugs with rouge
thinking about maybe
what you'll do for dinner
read the paper real slow
coffee & pie
it feels
so good
dreaming about that beer that paper
while you're stacking those
damned crates & checking them
against the bill
of lading
it almost makes you
horny
if you don't watch out

VALENTINE

I told you
I had nothing to offer
beyond what you could see
but you didn't pay me any mind
& the next morning you're already up,
quiet as a shoplifter,
regarding my prints
like accusers caught in lies,
eyeing my closets as if severed limbs
were concealed in the shelves,
your ear cocked, tapping the walls
for hidden safes, secret passageways,
whatever it is a woman can determine
from sounds a man stops noticing
the first time his woman moves on.
While I shaved, you stepped
out of your jeans & curled
your thigh into mine, pressed
your lips just beneath my ear,
& watched fresh blood streak my jaw
like warpaint before whispering
our late breakfast could wait later still.
It is too soon for pet names
so we'll hold our tongues,
but when you straddle down over me,
the sweat on our foreheads
beading like dew, let's sit up,
our shoulders squared, & stare
into the mirrors of each other's eyes
like honest bargainers
& see who smiles first.

CANDY

before we undressed
you said your nipples
were like chocolate
and I prayed they
would melt in my mouth
and not in my hands
because I would hate to
stop and lick my fingers

oh be

at least human in the night
if in the day ·
you must wear a face
official as the noon sun

in the night
be on your knees
or weep for your mother
and let your eyes trace
the simple hunger in mine

LACE

That operatic Italian, the pink scrim
of his running shorts revealing
his muscular thighs
as he jogs by, I
want him, I want
the executive in his
yellow tie and blue blazer, the wrist corsage
of his gold Seiko watch which looks
also like a locket for the photo I am taking
of the shirtless
construction workers
wearing those jeweled bloodmarks,
their nipples. The whole avenue
of men, all the fabric
it takes to cover them! My heart,
that actress, beats
as though my chest were stage curtains
that would simply part
and allow her
to leap forth naked,
Isadora! I know

this is temporary, know
there are sour expressions
made necessary by hard thoughts
and by the bad smell
of these gingko trees. And I
could tell you this: my father
is dead twenty-three years, his shadow
like old newspaper
blown to a bare tree's branch, never
lifting; I have only last Friday
destroyed the shrine of a photograph
I carried in that triptych,

my wallet. Even today
with white shirts sailing
up and down the avenue
on those beautiful masts,
the bodies, the yawning world
swallows everything we've loved
and then insists, to make it worse,
on publishing full-color postcards
which picture those lost objects
and we comply by writing
"Wish you were here" over and over
with mixed feelings. The costumes

of moods are worn directly
one over the other
so that walking around
with nothing to do
we hear the rustle of many
multi-colored slips.
Yet as I glide down the flower-laden aisle
of the crowded street, eyeing
what I would like to buy, those great
tight pants that might flatter me but which
more importantly I might flatter
by recalling, I stitch
the effort of my attention
into this lace
which wafts behind me, white
train of a bride.

GIFT

Make it the tart wine on your lips
Make it the cream sweet and full in your mouth
Make it your breasts cupped in your palms
Make it the thicket of darkness between your thighs
Make it a fever swelling in your hands
Make it an unbearable heat
Make it rise into the wet darkness
Make it dangerous
Make it explode from desire
Make it the first crowning when you broke through into light
Make it the light radiant and new

The
place I
started
from

BERNARD AND SARAH

"Hang them where they'll do some good," my grandfather
said, as he placed the dusty photograph
in my father's hands. My father and I stared
at two old people posed stiffly side by side—
my great-great-great-grandparents, in the days
when photography was young, and they were not.
My father thought it over as we drove home.

Deciding that they might do the most good
somewhere out of sight, my father drove
a nail into the back wall of his closet;
they have hung there ever since, brought out
only on such occasions as the marriage
of one of his own children. "I think you ought
to know the stock you're joining with" he says.

Then back they go to the closet, where they hang
keeping their counsel until it is called for.
Yet, through walls, over miles of fields and woods
that flourish still around the farm they cleared,
their eyes light up the closet of my brain
to draw me toward the place I started from,
and when I have come home, they take me in.

HOME FOR THANKSGIVING

The gathering family
throws shadows around us,
it is the late afternoon
of the family.

There is still enough light
to see all the way back,
but at the windows
that light is wasting away.

Soon we will be nothing
but silhouettes: the sons'
as harsh
as the fathers'.

Soon the daughters
will take off their aprons
as trees take off their leaves
for winter.

Let us eat quickly—
let us fill ourselves up.
The covers of the album are closing
behind us.

BODIES OF WATER

Here on Michigan Avenue,
this is for Jasmyn,
whose family has never seen the midwest
or been to a beach
or flown on a plane.
And whose mom is named Erie,
after the lake,
and her mom's sister,
the aunt she doesn't like,
named Superior.
There should be brothers, twins,
one a brooding wanderer,
the other a computer programmer.
Huron, and Ontario.
Imagine all of them, out of their element,
swimming and swimming in darkness,
muscular arms outstretched under the moon.
Imagine the shadows, each in formation,
one by one striking pavement
as they strive, landlocked, toward water.

THE BLOOD TREE

1. *Annie*

Not without fear
I begin her journey backwards
from Ellis Island to Vilna,
expecting nothing and all
that she was and could still give me,
no matter if I had to tear up
grasses, roots, tubers with my bare hands.
Where at 15 she faced the dark English brick,
having stepped into London's ghetto
at Saint Catherine's Pier.
I look through bombed-out windows
and the plum-dark eyes from Bangladesh
for a sign of my grandmother's
mysterious lover, from whom she had to flee
to New York and, most indirectly, to me;
look for a line from the story. The Story—
until I must place them both
outside the crumbling House for the Jewish Poor
and once again, once again, invent the past.

2. *Gittel*

Shaking in a thin orange sweater
inside her dank Vilna flat:
skin-and-bones Gittel, old as the century.
Her shabby blue eyes fill with tears
when she hears I am American, a *scheine madel*;
holds me so tight I will never make
the boat to Ellis Island
and my grandmother's life.
Gittel, who never made the journey;

Gittel, who has never tasted an orange;
Gittel, who has outlived everything—
Der Krieg, the camps, the clenched
Soviet jaws, two husbands, six children—
Gittel, who has outlived everything but herself
and will soon share the bloody Lithuanian earth
with potatoes and pale carrots,
still dreaming of an America
where oranges fall freely from the trees
into silver buckets near the Brooklyn Bridge.

3. *Digging Potatoes in Svencionys*

Rich earth but few potatoes,
mostly marble-size, and the beets
like a baby's fist. They blame the drought.
Elsewhere in Lithuania the wheatfields
already burn, join to make flames
that devour even the cabbage flowers
and the wooden houses
painted impossible citrus colors,
burning again what has so many times
been burnt—the market, the music,
all five synagogues, the memories,
the forests that even now ring with shots
and blinding screams,
the places that were the places
that were the places.

4. *The Blood Tree*

So many bodies
dumped dead and alive
the earth danced in disbelief
when the blond young guards
hastily shoveled mud several feet
to conceal unspeakable shame,
eight-thousand killed in an hour,
the blond guards laughing and drinking
in the forest near Svencionys.
Blumka, my friend, who has outlived
so much pain that nothing hurts—
not the bunions and thick purple veins,
not the space where the heart was—
Blumka bends to kiss the place
where perhaps are her mother's bones
under the dirt, the weeds, the wild flowers.
She points out to me
the witness and guardian tree;
I tear off some of its bright red bark.
Perhaps below the soft mound with its flowers
and moss lie people of my own blood.
Perhaps. Perhaps not.
If I cannot find the roots the bark must do.

5. *Journeys*

All journeys are but one journey,
no matter when or where.

From the first lights off the Irish coast
to the last blink of receding sky
from whatever window it appears,
shuts its eye.

Memories assert themselves,
brief rivulets of music
on an old wireless; merge
to make a score.

Now a creek outside Vilna, 1992,
makes a chord with a creek
in Mount Fern, New Jersey, 1940.
A gypsy fiddle joins
a Greek shepherd's flute,
the rain of Svencionys joins the rain
that fell a century ago
on Jacob and Annie and their seven children
packing for America, to make possible
my own journey, though my very being
was less probable than a dream.
Rain joins with rain
and the entire journey flows out to sea,
mingles with all the other journeys,
theirs, mine, yours, the moon's.

MENU

I am off guard
when Mother is caught

in a gray halo, as her cigarette
makes its entrance. All her fire

is gone except for one lit
cinder still burning her life.

For years, she taught
me to eat her salmon timbales,

Swiss chard, and mince
pie. She never tired

of baking rolls, twice-risen,
buttered with the shining silver knife.

Now, I see she is hungry
and believe I can feed her,

fill her up, the way
a dream fights to hold you

long after the choke
of waking.

THE REDBUD, THE MAPLE AND
THE CHERISHED YARD

The redbud, the maple and the cherished yard,
the memory that will not erode:
that tree, the swings in the corner by the fence,
the redbud pushing its pale petals towards
the split sky: all these belie
the family's dark edge, the mother's flights,
father's gifts to daughter
in the dark. How she rode those swings by the maple
hoping to escape him, how she
wished the sky to swallow her, the young girl pumping
legs to push the fast swing faster, crying as her arc
returned her to the starting point

The pink dress he adored her in
ruffled and pale like redbud with the mother
gone and the low lights like firefly
he'd take her hand and hand
her something secret something mommy
mustn't know about and in the darkness even it
was like the redbud
flowers, rosy, pale, falling all
away, flowering again next spring

MULDOON, WIDOWER

once there was a man
who had his heart extracted
at seven in the morning

for the first twelve hours
he hardly felt it

then he went into his closet
and wept noisily
among the jackets and neckties

unaware
his child came
to put her arms around him

they fell asleep
watching the news

SPREE

It was twenty thousand
by one account, forty
by another. But when
Uncle Dave's dad died,
he and Aunt Anna took
off for the city to
spend. They leased
a suite in the Jefferson
for six months, drank
till they ran out of
friends, then to Atlanta
for six more. Anna
danced naked on tables.
Once they found Dave
propped up plastered
in bed in Anna's gown.
When a year and the
money were gone, they
came back to town.
Dave became main-
tenance man at
the library, swept
hard marble floors,
remembered carpeted
halls. Neither he
nor Anna ever looked
sad after that. He
died an Elder in the
Church, she later
quietly.

ALZHEIMER'S #1

We move from the known to the
unknown, but this is a vulgar twist,
caravans of disguise

surround us: your face, home,
    family—
forgotten familiars. You sit and
    stare,
wander and drift, not a ship riding
    the

sea's broad back, but a dingy,
    without
sail or wind.

Could I give you an anchor,
something to hold you
in a place that digs

to the bottom of "past,"
the floor of memory, I would. But
you keep sinking as I grasp for the
    ring,

stock, shank of your life—
something to slip a knot through,
a way to tie you to ancestors, or

a single progenitor!

But in this place that is
neither here nor there,
you are forsaken by days

that have been your own,
and years honored in pictures
and other emblems of love
are the wind passing through an
    old one's

thin grey hair 'til all is life we
    cannot
hold from Time's undertow. Still
    never
full of estrangement, I will seek
    you,

will surrender you only to the eye
    of Love,
face of earth, or the heat of
stars, if only for one moment more.

TOUR OF DUTY

Back from the funeral, he finds himself
going down into his father's basement again
on his own dare, and does not turn on the lights
in remembrance of the fear he had once felt.
There is that empty coal chute
in the corner where the devil hung out
tools lashed to a pegboard: the Black
and Decker drill and router,
the soldering iron that melted
metal into beaded sweat, and sump pump
standing in shame in its own dark water.
In the center, like an underground oak,
grown fat and sullen in its disuse,
the furnace they had thrown him in,
then turned a crank, and did not
hear his pounding on the walls,
but turned up the heat.

When they had let him out,
his father hugged him like a prodigal
and had a feast, failing to notice
he had ground down all his teeth,
saying "You have singed a little, son,"
and kicked him up the stairs to bed
and wondered why he stayed there,
and stayed there for months
drinking cold six packs and watching
waves of snowflakes on the television.

A workbench is like a place
on which a kicking body is flung.
Surgery and sacrifice, he has known them both,
and knows the law that says a son must

let a father go untroubled into death
but he has let his finger warm the cold
drill's trigger, smelled the band
saw stalling on the bone,
and wishes the old man had stuck
around a little more to trouble some.

GENESSEE STREET

Suddenly, the blue-tiled doorway
and Mrs. Graham, our matron landlady,
whose keys would unlock cellar
storage bins with black widow spiders.

The last door
was my grandparents'. They take me in.
Sarah, ferociously sewing, baking.
David, Romanian gypsy.

Sarah has the double pull-out bed
in the front room, David and I
the back bedroom. Now, the night
bedroom door blows

open a cellar suffocating
with David's breath. The only light,
draped with an old shirt.
His bed and mine, arm's distance.

My mother, alone in her flat
on the floor above us, yawns,
inspects her nail polish,
puffs the bed pillows while

hands like giant spiders
travel my skin. The arched back heaves
its shadow onto the wall.
A wet mouth on mine of stone.

VISIT TO THE CEMETERY

1

At the cemetery gate a sea of gravestones,
unending rows stretch for miles.
Reluctant to look, the angle of my retina
skewed, eyelids fluttering, lens misty,
the first inscription: *Semen Wander,*
cherished husband. Bald, smiling, rimless gold
spectacles. Jewish law forbids graven images
even photographs? Has a spurned mistress glued it on?

At the family plot, carved stone inscriptions:
Jacob Widder, beloved father, 1883-1968,
Blanche Widder, wife and mother, 1891-1962.
I'd almost forgotten the dates
My brother visits, sees to the care,
and I contribute in perpetuity. White
wild flowers, impatiens, sometimes
called jewelweed, scatter their seed.
In April at my ninety-two year old aunt's

funeral, the last of that generation,
ten years of Parkinson's, embarrassed
by disease, a blessing, they said.
A closed coffin, scarecrow body,
splintered bones. A year later,
the unveiling
Place rocks on the grave
Stones fix the soul's compass.
An end to restless wandering
in the silence of the tomb.

2
Earth to earth, dust
to dust, an incantation
The orthodox wrap the dead
in muslin, the rabbi says,
bury them in mounds of dirt,
say a prayer for the soul's
transmigration.
Aunt Marie's great grandchildren
play leap frog over the grave.

The game of life continues,
we squeeze pleasure from a fist,
fill epicurean appetites,
life begins with a tangled
umbilical cord. Mourning
stops time, breaks the hour glass,
sand spills on the ground.
However bruised, hope quickens
its pace even for the old.

3
Humpty Dumpty's fall left him a hunchback.
When we play hide-and-seek noone wants to be it.
No peace in longing, no pleasure in hedonism,
memory gnaws at us like an empty belly.
I hold my father's hand on the deck of a cruise ship,
together we spray the dogwood at the front door.
Whenever I scraped my knee as a child, my father
said, "You'll forget it by the time you marry."
Twice married since, knives are sharp, cuts

don't heal without skin grafts, the premonition
of loss continuous as Chinese water torture.

In my will, I shall leave beauty and power
to the black panther, fertility and speed
to the spotted cheetah, unfinished poems
to whoever wants them. Love is clean hair,
artfully combed.

A star-filled sky, Ella Fitzgerald on tape,
sings *Someone to Watch Over Me*.
In the last scene of the play, the two
remaining hostages, symbolically, like Spartans
leaving for battle, comb each other's hair.

BLOOD TIE

Cousin Bobby broke every window in the chicken house
grampa tanned his hide but he chewed his licorice
jawbreakers and laughed that throaty laugh I knew was
crackers for all that I'd never heard the word schizoid
            But I want him back alive though mad

He pushed Sis and me into the cowshit and was pushed there
in turn by Mom but he did not cry he never cried never never
            I want him back though dead

He and I were put to scooping gravel along the river for
Dad's new cattle barn our team those dappled Percheron
grays as big as apple trees they stamped at flies and
watched as Bobby wanting to drive grabbed the lines
and whipped me in my eyes
            I want him back alive

Bobby hit me in the eyes fifty years ago while the horses
stood silent and without shame you know animals have no
future they are innocent of anxiety too and they do not
wish for return of the dead
            But I want him back

I almost killed Bobby that day pushing at his windpipe
with my thumbs till his eyes bugged out and his torn shirt
spotted with cough-hawked blood
            I want him back

Even there in South Chicago where he earned a living
painting houses till 1957 when he got sent up for auto
theft and served two-and-a-half because he had a rap
sheet as long as your arm
            But I want

After he was sprung he stopped by my Aunt Margaret's but
she refused him a stake and he cursed her and went on
up the road walking and never came back
        I want

TOUCH

We all want to touch,
in some picture of our father's lives,
a miracle of love bigger
than a Cecil B. DeMille finale,

an image more real than the hot
plastic feel of an old Chevy
racing the Manhattan skyline
to Brooklyn, a cold wife and dinner.

Stronger than his rough voice
or hand riffling your hair…
Father's hand in mine,
his holding grandfather's,

sons letting loose without a thought.
One by one each reaches back
through the dusty glass
for one last confirming touch.

PASSING

A professor invited me to his college class. They were
reading Larson's *Passing*. One of the black
students said, "Sometimes light-skinned blacks
think they can fool other blacks,
but I can always tell," looking
right through me.
After I told them I am black,
I asked the class, "Was I passing
when I was just sitting here,
before I told you?" A white woman
shook her head desperately, as if
I had deliberately deceived her.
She kept examining my face,
then turning away
as if she hoped I'd disappear. Why presume
"passing" is based on what I leave out
and not on what she fills in?
In one scene in the book, in a restaurant,
she's "passing,"
though no one checked her at the door—
"Hey, you black?"
My father, who looks white,
told this story: every year
when he'd go to get his driver's license,
the man at the window filling
out the form would ask,
"White or black?" pencil poised, without looking up.
When my father remained silent, the man
would look up at my father's face.
"What do you think
he would always write?" my father'd say.

AFTER WORDS

All these days of her burying,
bits of well-meant chicken and fruit
stick in my throat—clumps of unsaid words
jumbled with those shouted long ago.
Once, grounded a week for coming in late,
she climbed out her window,
slept all night in a field.
                          At supper,
her usual time to call, each chance
ring of the phone pulls me up like a puppet.
In dreams, I wade waist-deep in slurry, her voice
rising and falling ahead of me—an unmistakable
print on a sonograph.
                          Stories I've saved
fill my whole body. My mouth opens of itself,
begins to shape our secret jokes as if her head
would turn. Sometimes she's at her old desk,
dialing a toy telephone, each number
circling back. She stays on hold for hours
as I try to match an American phone
to a foreign plug, but the cord hangs
slack.
             Last night the scene changed,
almost worth the wait for sleep—
four boys in the car that killed her
were chasing us. She outwitted them,
sneaking into a house and out the back.
While they searched the cellar, she jumped
on her bike, I held on behind. We sped down
a brambled path, chattering like schoolgirls,
knowing we had a lead.

BEDDING DOWN

I circle patches of graves and potted mums,
wind the borders to her fresh-cut stone.
Tracing her name, I picture her at four,
pretending sleep beneath the petaled garden
of grandmother's quilt. The corners of a grin
begin to play against the silence of her face
as she waits for me to tap her arm, magic godmother
bringing cocoa topped with cream.

I dig my fingernails into this soil.
It moves easily. My mind opens
the car's trunk, grabs any tool—
the tire wrench fits my hand.
Piling the rumpled grass,
I dredge through layers of clay,
tear off the crimped sheet to quiet her shivers,
massage her stiff arm until it wakes.

GRANDFATHER'S FAVORITISM

My uncle Yuen suspected his father
of favoritism, even from the grave.
Bull-headed men, they never gave,
wanted only to dominate. Uncle forbade
Mother to visit their father's grave
with food and other offerings needed
by the Chinese dead, in case she got
a larger share of ancestral luck.

My mother obeyed his injunction for four
years, till she dreamt her father in rags,
housed in a mud hut with holes for window
and door, his needs forgotten by his son.
That week she made a bonfire in our yard,
by its flames, dispatched a paper mansion,
furniture, a million Bank of Hell dollars
to Mr. Au Sang, c/o Ghost Village.

Later, she dreamt him happy in his new house.
My uncle visits once a year. He blames
her still for parental love he couldn't win.

SPRING ROLLS

Cecile, Saigon doctor's daughter, wanted
to elope with her dashing foreign suitor.
Her father made them stay six months
so Cecile could learn to cook,
her fiancé learn to wait.
In '64 he took her home to Germany
where she cleaned her house herself,
perfected what the family cook had taught her,
traveling to Paris each month
for lemon grass, rice paper, *nuoc mam*.
Years later I watched her cook spring rolls
fried crisp and light;
pork pounded thin, garlic-grilled;
cabbage and carrot and cucumber salad.
Like a garden: all balance and contrast:
hot spice relieved by cool crunch;
soft bite of rice vinegar against
tidy texture of rice vermicelli.
I never thought I couldn't go back,
she said, her voice like almond oil.
Why were Americans so half-hearted...
She looked at me and then away.
Father died five years ago,
someone in Paris said. My letters go
unanswered, but my packages don't come back,
she went on, waiting
for me to help myself to more.

THE FORGIVENESS DEVICE

"Hold the flashlight still."

But I can't.
I'm only a child and I watch
as he puffs up bigger and bigger
—like a barrage balloon—
pushing back his glasses
that are smeared with grease
as he winds the clicking
ratchet again and again
changing sparkplugs in the dark.

The garage light won't reach outside
to where we stand around the
burgundy Chrysler. I'm scared.
Snot dripping down my face. Tears.
The fender is too big for me
to lean over, but I try
and my arm is so numb
it tingles. The drop light
flickers against the hood.
My father is stripping the skin
off his knuckles as the ratchet
slips and dings off the manifold.
He's talking to himself.
Saying he can't see and
beginning to cuss.

I realize now—
that he's angry at himself,
at his failure to fix
something so elementary
and his anger

is misdirected at me.
But back then I was just
a bookish little kid
afraid of failing.
I didn't know yet that
it's okay to fail.
That my father was
just trying to save a buck
and afraid of aging.
But the price was high.

Why can't you wait till morning?
I wanted to say, but didn't dare.
He drinks another Ballantine,
crumples the can and drops
it on the driveway.

If I could
I'd materialize at that exact moment
the aluminum still rattling
against the concrete.
Tell him, "It's not that important Dad.
It's just a couple of sparkplugs.
Don't get so stressed."
I'd rub my red bandanna
across his forehead
and soothe his brow.
Tell him, "Relax."
And watch his features soften.
Hear that laughter again.

And I'd forgive him.
I really would.

An
unknown
withered
hour

AT ODDS

On my own, I misplace your keys,
am unable to straighten the desk
or grasp one thought entire.

It is just as difficult to sleep
with your half of the bed
weighted and bare.

This morning I found
your Madras shirt,
the one you wore

the hottest days of August,
beside your suits wrapped
still from the cleaners.

Tell me, what
will I do with these,
what will I do in winter.

PATCH

You wake, feeling okay,
reach for the old touch
that roughs your lips
and curls your fingers,
then the bright yellow day
pries open your brain:
gone, gone, gone, gone.

How, how, your throat sighs,
can you make coffee much
less drink it read the paper
walk the dog draw eyes
on your bare face dress
drive talk on the phone?
Gone, gone, gone, gone.

You know you could
put on that good black suit
go to a restaurant brood
over a sherry before
and a coffee after but
the waiter would know
you were alone. Gone, gone

your lacy veil, your
dangerous fangs, the curl
of your lip that burned
the world to ashes
in your yellow hand. Howl
Macbeth: "Patch, be gone."
(It sticks to your wishbone.)

BLAZING ACCUSATION

(In racial upheaval in Birmingham, Alabama, 1963,
four young girls died in the blasting of a church.)

Too early a death for those who young
have lost prophecy in blast and flame.
The broken have been assembled
as best could be to pose for burial.
The man in bleak authority intones
the word that cannot tell
when last the girls stood singing
under the sweetest tree,
how remote from nightmare
they giggled secrets believing
death was the end for the old.

After the moans are choked
and the flowers gone petalless,
the girls will be with greatgrandparents,
themselves not long in that last room.
Mothers and fathers,
grandfathers and grandmothers
still pace the waking street
though few are the footfalls
that echo where the children lie.

But walk they will
the sixty-odd more years they're due.
Beyond allotted time and self
the four of them will go

down red gullies of guilt
and alleys of dark memories,
through snagging fields of scarecrows,
and up an unforgetting hill
to blazon accusation of an age.

THE KING OF A RAINY COUNTRY

"Je suis comme le roi d'un pays pluvieux"
Baudelaire

In my kingdom where rain
never ending, quiet as a blade
between two ribs, slips in
to quell the surgings of a heart
still unruly, in this palace draped
with ennui like grey silk,
where tarnished mirrors yawn, opaque
stagnant ponds no animal drinks from,
the ladies of the court bare pink breasts
to the crown on my head with avid boredom,
glide into my bed—a rosary of pearls
smooth and untouched under my hand,
their cool flesh unquenching
as the memory of water.

Here we only embark
for grey Cytheras. At times, in chase
of an elusive joy, we play Petit Trianon
in the stables, writhe trysts in the hay,
doomed needle seekers, on an empty quest.
Even the sad eyes of the horses,
that accept all, the warm
cloud of their breath can't heal me.

Because it's then, in the spent calm
of never ending rain on a tin roof
that comes the echo of other possibilities,

a land of storms and violent sunsets
of brilliant blues that bleach the earth,
scour it clean. A vein of water, lifeline
on the palm of a hand. And of a woman
with severe brow and quiet eyes,
whom I shall never know
but waits for me, and judges and forgives me.

SIGNS

I thought while I struggled with
a splinter tonight, hunched over and
consumed with the aim of tweezers:
That's what we
concern ourselves with,
making sure we are free of
aches, that our bodies are working for us
    we believe ourselves part of the order
    of self-preservers, blessed
    by nature herself

like a newt, given the signal
to follow her male, lay her eggs
in the place she herself was born,
crawl out of the water and
leave the sac to burst open—
she makes her way
colored
like damp leaves

her purpose over.
Is she satisfied then?

A blue jay dives upward sharply,
flashes its scaled belly at my window.
I close my eyes to the flash
but its colors do not remind me
of a revelation, or bits of human wisdom
drawn from other wings.

And this loss I feel
this cave in me as black as
the low-humming danger of stories—
    I want the spice of the bay trees to tell me its place,
    I want to sap the brambles of their magic
    and begin to understand.

GROANING BED

I tell you, something is always
dying in this damnable place;
each day the green fruit turns
deep, gives up its heavy harvest,
breaks down its home.

      Awaiting your return
I watch cucumber leaves white
with disease flutter and hang
from their trellis. In the fall
shadow, moss roses turn
their timeless clocks
toward an unknown withered hour.

Weeds crowd in. They mob the dark's
cabaret. Nightshade burlesques
the eggplant petal and melon flower;
these blossoms, so soon cast off
by their fruit.

Since you've gone, how cluttered
the garden grows! Congregated marigolds
force carrot ferns to the ground—
the zinnia row, a small society
where one gold imitates another.

        *

      It's for you, this offering!
Once a scattering of seeds, now
mysterious heartaches of the eggplant;
tomatoes bowed, weighted, waiting
to be gathered, so much good to save,
so much sweetness still to savor.

Come home. Let's clear the bed.
of those who starve us: all
the fathers   the mothers
children within—
all who shout and wrestle
with our lives
on the groaning bed.

DRIVING ON EMPTY

She's lifted her face,
reduced her bust, tried
hypnosis to lose

her passion for country
breakfasts and double fudge.
She's compared herself

to the child-women
he likes to fix cars for—
skinny waitresses from Waldorf

in smirking eye-shadow.
Knows what they look like—
stole the film once

from his Instamatic. He took
pictures on the boat.
She continues to compare

herself until her cells
whirl off-kilter, three-
quarters of her stomach

slips under the knife.
The oncologist hunts
the nodes.

It's after chemo,
when she is not quite
ready for a hospice,

she sees Jack make a pass
at the visiting nurse,
slip a fifty in her purse.

A psychic told her once:
"You will live to be
ninety

and find a second husband
who truly loves you."
One day he asks her to sign

two blank checks
"just in case."
She rallies, enraged,

but it doesn't last.
Morphine drips
through the hole in her chest.

She is too weak to protest,
or doesn't care,
he is there for her last breath.

Unable to face her dead,
or her friends,
he squelches plans for a service.

He takes the ashes home
and places the urn
on the mantle

under the mirror he uses
to fix his tie,
smooth his stubborn cowlick.

It's not as much fun
fooling around,
now she's gone.

He's never liked to be alone.
Between sex and valium
it's hard to choose.

Just outside the window
is her feeder for the birds.
He takes to sitting where

she used to sit for hours,
sometimes with tears
he's at a loss to explain.

anger

some days it
enters the house

without gazing
at the flowers.

perhaps it has already traipsed
through gardens smelling

of smoked coca plants,

or wild irish rose petals
planted by brothers like earl,

who taught me the chords to
"purple haze."

now his face is blank
manuscript paper.

or it is etched with
riffs

i cannot sing with him.

but working does not
change

the rapidly
descending melody

which begins
the moment i leave

my office.

and wait for buses
that are late,

ragged,

or do not come.

THE SUICIDES

There is much confusion about
the suicides: those who reject
us. It is those who take dark as an end

in itself who have that claim. They put
the finger of darkness on all motion
towards or away, and on the changes

of blood or sun. They have conquered
nature, where every insect, tiger, crab
fights death, this being the sole passion

shared absolutely. Which beast
rejects life? The hound, grieving
to death is only craving fresh

life for his master. And we call
suicides those for whom the tunnel
of possibility has narrowed, closes

before them. A gracious couple
enamored of life came to that tunnel's
end, and like Etruscan figures

lay side by side. They wanted
nothing so much as life. No;
the suicides belong to each other,

fraternal in solitude—
A rage of hunger for the void,
a shared lust for zero.

Being exclusively human, this is
like all humans, mysterious.
Without inducement the beasts live

to live. Often "he/she had everything
to live for," we say. This is the thing
itself; exclusively human. Authentic.

MARIA

When the small sun yawns,
and creeps back in the maples,
I will tell you the story
of my own Nicaragua,
when I sat, rocking,
in the wobbled light
of one kitchen candle—
then, two, in cruddy boots and uniform
smashed in the door,
scattering curled feathers
where I was mending a pillow.
My hands were tied,
buttons sliced from my dress,
my breasts shivering
and all the while I could not tell
because the curved moon held
like the policeman's machete
because only the woman knows
how to clench her teeth
and bay like a wolf…
my husband, knee deep
whacking sugar canes in the field,
bundling them back
in the truck,
how could he know
what was happening on the porch
before the shot rang out
as I reeled and fell back
to the earth,

tasting its grit, its salt:
because now it was flesh
because he didn't ask for mercy
because it was his hunger,
moaning my name,
in God's hollow breath,
moaning the way he would
when he lay on top of me,
stinking of tobacco
wrists nailed to my wrists,
lips to my lips,
tongue to tongue,
this is my story,
the last word of my love
sweating through darkness:
whispering Maria, Maria
bush of my blood,
here is another fruit of my cock,
another paradise, fluttering   in.

AFTER DEATH

Your virtues were a level fertile field:
I did respect your strength and I was grateful
for your gentleness. But oh, my dear,
the fissures of your faults, your crevices,
your peaks of doom gave contour to your soul.
It was your very sins, if such they were,
that made you need me—wakening me to love.

If you are heavened, I am doubly helled.
I need you still: your need of me is done.
I'm like a goblet filled with cooling water,
shaped for cradling hands, the touch of lips.
I'm brimmed for quenching—and there is no thirst.

LOVE POEM

When you take my breast in your hand
my breathing deepens until it is as if
all my pores are open to take you in.
Once I wanted enormous breasts to feed
everyone. I have not lost that feeling
altogether, the wish to feed everyone,
but I am proud of small breasts. I hope
they do not disappear under a knife, under
some misguided cell. Someplace deep
inside these angles that make up me,
the thought of you can soothe me, can make
my insides leap with joy, even now when
you leave over and over for places you
need to be, without me. If I knew how
to keep you with me, I would do whatever
needed to be done. I think I would. I
will have no chance to prove it. You have
gone, slipped over the edge of my life
and I had no way to hold onto your hand,
though I wanted to. I can feel your hand
holding mine. I press my one hand with
the other and imagine it is your hand again
holding mine. Two lost souls, you called us,
and I listened, laughing, not believing you.
Now I believe you. The delight you gave me
held off the bitter hatred that came on,
fought it off as if it were a saving knight,
straight out of some myth I couldn't manage
to make up for myself. You were real and earnest
and adoring just long enough to save my life
and I thank you for it. Somewhere here I

will always love you. Love your hands, your
lines and your voice, reading what you write
will stir me in ways you cannot know. When
you walk into a room where I am, my blood
will leap, even as it always has, before
you even knew my name. And when you speak
it, my name, I would be yours forever if only
you wanted me. But there is no forever,
and the me you might have wanted is lost
still wandering about in some forest or other,
gazing at her palms and wondering who she is
or might have been.

IMPASSE

Because I can't tell you
what wind did to the roof,

how hard young Melvin plays lacrosse
or those reasons the doctor gave,

I write to you and about you,
use words as leeches. At times

the need to look up and quote
to you from a page is so great,

the prohibition strong,
I am like an overfull diary

bound with twine, thoughts fixed
and nearly as unspoken as yours.

BONING KNIFE

The right tools
Make the task easier.
There's a fine heft
To this knife.
It will take flesh
From frame cleanly,
Keep colors of scales
From swimming into new life,
As surely as the blade
Of your caution
Keeps your need
From my bones,
Lest joined
They take on
A life of their own.

An undertow of dream and exile

THE STARS OF THE BEAR

"Vaghe stelle dell'Orsa"
Leopardi

I

November. A huntress moon stalks her prey
across the nitid sky—where a small star
freezes, rabbit ensnared by headlights—
looking for a kill, clean, and round
and perfect as herself. But the She-Bear
sleeps in another hemisphere tonight,
hibernates in the past as in her cave
of ice—and fears no arrows
nor unleashed remembrance.

II

I'm five, the night of my birthday,
barefoot in the garden and someone
says: "Look, look at the bears!
Can you see them?" as I search the sky
for a great muzzle, a strong paw
hooking a salmon in the Milky Way
like the bear in my book, who likes
fish and blackberries. But I can only
see stars, thousand galactic fireflies
dancing above my head, a stellar vertigo
rotating, abyss that sucks me in
so that I must bend and clutch the grass
by my feet or I shall fall into the sky.
And then I see them, the bear and her cub,
the wondrous menagerie of the void
parade under the big tent, starry fur

twinkling electric, heavy bodies
asway with the music of the spheres,
around and around, till they merge
in a jumble of stars, disappear—
as if it had been all a trick, worse,
a lost paradise. For the first time
I taste exile.

III

And does it ever end, this sensing
that it should have been different,
the fruit not eaten, the right path
easier to recognize? The trees
had no sign posts and the she-wolf,
the lion and the lynx have become
fellow travelers. The selva oscura
goes the way of rain forests—soon
there'll be no trees in Madagascar
and Polaris no longer shows the way.
Constellations revolve in horoscopes
in the morning paper—those easy promises,
eclipsed by the headlines. Another war,
some bridge has collapsed into a river
turbulent as its twin, time
gone and remembered. The past
is snared in a net of stars,
present and lost like the Great Bear.

WHAT A PENNY BOUGHT

The vise of Mr. Sexton's arm
tightened around my waist,
hoisted me up
above the glass counter, high enough
to stare into the round
mouth of the giant Mason jar,
past peppers and cloves bobbing
on the surface, to the dark
muck beneath
which even shafts of sunlight
failed to penetrate: the place
I'd seen long knobby
creatures hiding, submerged
side by side, across each other.

I held my breath
against the gusts of vinegary air
and dipped in one shy finger,
slowly, until Mr. Sexton
hiked me up another
inch or two, his voice
grunting *hurry, boy,*
and pick one. And then I did,
plunged my whole arm
deep into cool slime, my hand
opening, fitting at last

around the prize I pulled out: firm
fleshy pickle, its ooze

dripping on my shirt, on Mr. Sexton,
across the counter
and linoleum floor. Outside,
between bites, I licked my fingers
one by one as sky
and clouds, the distant
hills all flared up
reckless and green.

DE EXILIO Y AMARGURA

Quiero comerme el sol a gajos esta tarde,
y reventar en el aire mi pasado;
quiero reir hasta el fondo de mis huesos,
y sacudirme cadenas con la risa.

Pero recuerdo a mi gente que pelea
y se sacude cadenas con las ganas
de comerse de una vez el sol a gajos
y despertarse al aire del futuro.

Yo, náufraga de exilio y sin tibiezas,
deliro lejos del sol y de mi gente.

EXILE AND BITTERNESS

This afternoon I want to feast on slices of sunlight
and blow away my past into the air;
I want to laugh so hard my bones hurt,
and shake off my chains with the laughter.

But I remember my people fighting back,
shaking off their chains with the same desire
to devour without let-up slices of sunlight
and wake up breathing the air of the future.

I, shipwrecked by exile and without warmth,
rave delirious far from the sun and my people.

THE CANDY QUEEN

The fires under her black
pots burned out fifty years
ago, but I keep the red scale
with its four black weights
and her lollipop molds that hold
the odors of pineapple and cherry
butterscotch and raspberry
in shapes of running rabbit,
pony and fiddle, cornucopia
        and Kewpie doll.

Dream:
She is living in a tall-standing
burnt-sienna house, unlike
anything she ever inhabited.
She sits in an inglenook
with sister candy queens
and their teacher Mrs. Hannah
of the Candy Institute
the Mrs. Hannah who warned
Never wax your chocolates!
and extracted promises
from her pupils to choose
only one person to share
        their secrets.

I was my grandmother's chosen
apprentice—one who rarely
washed to the elbows; raider
of showcases, sneak thief
of marzipan and nougat—
one whose fingers tangled
the glassine bags, let slip
the aridor jar, scattered

the chocolate shot, rolled
the Roman punches round
not oblong; put pecans
on top of yellow bonbons,
almond slivers on mocha creams.

I come bearing a box
of miniature chocolates
waxed and shining, unworthy
gift for a queen.
I lay the box in her lap
as the candy queens avert
their eyes and Mrs. Hannah
shudders. Pensively
my grandmother gazes
at the candy…

In the days
of my failed bonbon dipping
she would say, "Never mind—
your talents lie elsewhere."

She always forgave me
my candy thieving, for she
too had the "sugar hunger"
and used to say, "If I'd been
a man, I'd have been a drinker."

I bid her good-bye, then turn
at the door, wondering if she
will cry me back as she used
to do in her last old days
but she waves me on.
Out the door and down the street
(and where will I ever find
that street, that house again)…

I think of the gift I should
have brought—a loaf of Irish
bread made by her hand-written
recipe, to show her that her yeast
keeps rising, ever rising
    in this grandchild.

GIBBOUS

I walk the local moon
like a Roman bishop,
purple hood, red gold,
ambling through the Curia.

Though I've prayed
the native Christian notion
of pain in these hills,
I have not kept
the cemetery from melting
into the river below.

*

For twenty years now
I've haunted these shores.
The dog tonight
who cannot control himself
and must be led by leash
is like an earlier, sweeter pet
sleeping under the pine
on the point. He is growing
grey—still, he would fetch
sticks in the river until
the cold seeped into his heart.

I am catching up to him,
dog years, human.
The wash of autumn.

*

I've walked with Hazard here.
The factory, "breathing our
distrust of darkness on the air"
has doubled in size.

Gypsy vandals trouble
the forest of our dreams.
The village is hiring a manager
to cope with the insomniac rust.

*

When I was a young man
my boots clacked against the cobblestone
as though I were turning the planet.
Now I am just a man
walking in solid shoes
under the moon.

You told me once
your very breath
was not yours for the keeping,
or the pleasure passing
through your loins.

The Town Hall and all
the records would slide off.
But I would stay, one of the
flints wrestled to the ground.

Suddenly, walking this ledge
is like riding a roller coaster.

*

I see it now,
the landscape that
caught and held you
under another full moon.
No need to trace roots.
The rich tapestry here
begins to feel as old
as Stonehenge, our love a huge
monolith rising in the garden.

I walk the black night
under the fair moon—
my old white dog—
the certainty I'd hoped for—
middle of my life—
blond dog fading—
winter landscape—
here, only here.

HOTEL BALTIMORE

We carve the night like a pineapple
talking of women we lost
without having said hello,
our laughter, a vocal restlessness,
the spirit within, a tenant
in the only building we own.

It is one thing to lose a job
quite another
to lose hope of a job.
Now we measure our lives in dog years:
for every pearl of Autumn
we age by seven,
no wonder then
we cherish what is timeless,
the pleasure of tropical fruit
in the dead of winter, the memory
of turning aside so you could
take off your gloves in private
finger by finger, the way
your nipple nested
in the strange oyster of my ear, how I
caressed you by believing
your every word.

It is one thing to lose a woman
quite another
to lose hope of a woman.
There is a hunger, a remorseful craving,
a limp that shows up forty years
after you turn an ankle.

It comes to this:
Brother you can keep your dime
but Sister can you spare your lips
or just
don't cross the street
when you see me coming.

INSOMNIA

The musical clock
the French chimes
call softly
through the ceiling
into my sleep.

I never heard them
before you came but
in the honey hours
after lovemaking
you called to me:
Listen, do you hear
the beautiful bells?

In this single bed
with extra blankets
I count the hours now
note by celibate note.

NOSTALGIA

Before all things
—antelope, giraffe,
atom, nebula—were named
in a lost place in the center
of histories and cities,
music and vocabulary
had not yet separated,
as the astronomers tell us
at the moment before creation
matter and energy had not yet
sundered to form the worlds.

If someone meant to convey
"water," the arterial pulse
of a powerful river,
or an ocean, the world's womb,
was hurled to the mind.

This is where we are always
longing to go, as if it were possible
to wander through
superimpositions of history
to a first garden,
where we will see each thing,
river, tree and fire,
before it was tamed with words,
and so create it for ourselves.
But we cannot yet reach this place,
for we are too young,
still warm and damp
with the afterbirth that accompanied

us into this world. Then it was
blood and placenta, and now
it is like the anemone-fingered ocean,
it stays with us forever,
an undertow of dreams.

I HAVE BEEN HUNGRY

Remember the bleeding rabbit
running the snow at sunset,
the sky pink, the snow blue,
the shadows blue in every footprint,
and pride in skill of aim
flayed me as that rabbit ran
its last full lope and fell and died.
We didn't fancy rabbit much,
beef or ham or chicken
mostly, not lamb, not
anything from sheep, can't get
the wool taste out of your mouth,
they said, believing it
was true because they'd believed
it so long.   But eating
that rabbit was almost
as hard as eating the old goats
we had for meat in 1932
when what it came down to
was the end of the farm.

MAPLE

Maple's not a street, a tree, it's a way
of seeing for Allie, TJ, and me.
It's the core, the bull's eye.

No one knows what we know.
When the factory starts up tomorrow morning,
and the cars drive down Main and Chestnut

and the newsstands run a brisk business,
and men crowd the counters of Lilly's Diner,
the horns and voices, bells and people

will blink open their rickety eyes.
But that's still another eight hours away.
See how the fake legs in the window

of the hospital supply store point inward
to their axis, stiff like a compass
that revolves around its center; and we revolve

around the pinched stars that hang
over our alley behind the Linton Superette
on Friday nights, and listen for the midnight train.

Later, we'll run like that, leaning forward,
fast as we can, our eyes closed. But for now,
it's enough, with Allie standing guard,

to make it with TJ inside a cardboard refrigerator box
and time ourselves, if we can, to explode
when the train's horn pulls us all

apart suddenly, and full of echoes.

LONE PINE

The wind peppered us that day, it raved like a lunatic
in the asparagus fern.
Affixed to nothing so much as everything

it circled, it landed (somewhere outside Miami) but the glide
forward just didn't seem to satisfy anymore.

There was that outhouse once with the half-moon
carved so precisely into it,
located behind the Fifties diner
shaped like a silver bullet in the picture postcard.
The garden and stucco wall surrounding the garden.
Tomatoes. A brilliant orangey-red, black and white
cows, animals who looked like us.

Ants covered the terra firma of the card like a canopy of dark
leaves and trillium, loads of trillium, so much we mistook it
for air.
A high whine, a buzzing
went up from the honeysuckle
installed beside the trompe l'oeil
of the pump handle like little moons.
The drip-drip of water in sunlight as if it were confetti.

True, there *was* a parade that day
and we had just missed it—wrapped up in each other,
the Two-Step, Tango, Peabody.

It had been a brief, a popular
time, it resembled nothing…something…coitus
interruptus. All our efforts gone into the supervision of it
before the evacuation like wasps from the burning nest.
There was sand and a long vertical drop, radical changes
in terrain. Knife-sharp ledges took it out on us;
a leap forward on the slippery track of time,
the smell of rubber tires burning.

We circled, we barnstormed in our bi-planes,
our bird-wings like a ball of wax
though mostly we imagined it.
For it was true we were poor
and could afford nothing... Nothing
afterall, was the name on the cover
of the autobiography that featured us.

It was a very fine day for looking at
the slides in the Viewmaster,
delicate as an illuminated manuscript
in the days before television... fragile almost
to the point of breaking.

We were dealing with what we felt.
Of course logic had no place in it.

Feelings are like pheromones—active in the air around us.

But there was that diner coffee to get through first,
music of the jukebox, a sense that what we were about
to say we had already said.
Only this time it was necessary to say it to each other:
before time ran out
before the charitable moments had been used up.

HELPMATES

I remember the train ride with the blind lady
where we each found out something about ourselves.
She asked me what *beautiful* means and if she
                                        looked that way.
I told her about the child who died in my arms
with an article stuck in her throat,
                        It was the word "I"
I told her about the baby who disappeared from the back
seat of the car where she had been playing —
When I picked her up I couldn't wipe the dirt from her face.
I told about the twins who were borrowed and how I feared
the new owners would take them and keep them in playpens
without their favorite snacks.
Where do the babies go when they grow?
Like trains out of the tracks they come
but where do they go?
She replied that at my age why did it matter.
She asked how people know what *beautiful* means.
                I told her that because of pain
in losing my children
my eyebrows grew together forming a beard.
She said if she didn't see it, it didn't happen
and to consider it all a passing fancy.

AMERICAN GOTHIC

Cold glace, accidentally placed in sunlight
The forest, the enchanted
stones.

The frost that winter
wept a dark rust, like Mt. Fuji
mourning its brothers in the next province.

                    We were always talking about

    "THE PROVINCES"—

running naked through the city, going broke.
The farm wiped out, the tractor
sold and the chickens,

    to make a living.

Days engulfed in a kind of
straitjacket (denim)

        of affairs,

of despair tied to the bedposts, the infrared
structures of the newly spangled evening.

Suddenly we owed more than we owned.
The dark cave of presentiment
had produced a jaundiced traffic of ideas
like confetti, like bells called
a sudden halt in the middle, say

before the song was over.

Consider the cities;
the nameless skies;

the fields running amok.
The highways like slack rope,
the children growing up beside them
and into their proverbial destinies like straw hats.

      Consider also the new

space-age poverty and
synonymous funk, the cool
droop to the shoulders.
The worn-out
cassette p!ayers, boom boxes, sealing rings
on mason jars.
The peaches, greenbeans,
pickled beets, and onions.

The plastic bags and
condoms; the highrises and condominiums.

      The pictures of

Niagara Falls:

      (bumper stickers really), on
      the cars, trailers, all over
      the lost luggage waiting
      for us at the airport.
The "Falls," rushing headlong into the "Grand Canyon."
Neckties hanging from the trees like shaved porcupines.

We offer these things little in the way of solace
a cool drink now and then

from the shallow well,
the reservoir out back.

REMEMBERING KEVAN MACKENZIE

Once upon a time I spent a summer
At a camp for children far from here,
Teaching riding to young boys and girls.
I taught them to make a horse go straight,
The way to make a horse stand still.
They grew and danced like weeds before my eyes.

Now there remains in my mind's eye
One face of all the faces of that summer;
It smiles at me, and I sit here
Wondering what's become of all the girls
That Kevan MacKenzie hounded straight
To earth, and may be chasing still.

Every week there was a dance, and still
I can recall the roll of those girls' eyes
As they hunted love, the first of summer:
Kevan, refusing to dance, stood straight
By the wall and dared the girls
To rout him from his sanctuary here.

Later he began to dress with care, and here
I remember the guarded gleam in his eye
As he came through the door and went straight
For the oldest and prettiest girl,
While with that stare that disturbs me still
The young girls hunted the first love of summer.

In the arms of that tall breath of summer
He danced, and looked her waist in the eye.
I whispered then, "Be cheerful, girls,

The sunshine boys are here."
When the music at last grew still,
The tall girl smiled, once more stood straight.

The days of dancing and love rode straight
To the last long week of that summer.
When I said goodbye to my boys and girls
I stood among them with tears in my eyes,
While Kevan MacKenzie, smiling still,
Said, "You must be glad to get out of here."

Now I sit here in another summer
And rising straight in my mind's eye
Kevan and his girls are dancing still.

WHAT IS SERVED

There must be an appetite for grief.
How else explain this gnawing on memory
until its bones are clean? The soul
barks and barks for its ration
of remembered things—the smell
of tangerines, undergarments stripped
like husks, exposing flesh as willful
and imperative. And how surrender
nourishes deliverance.
                          Now we are
swollen with absence and abstinence
tucks in our sheets. In our mouths
the aftertaste of satiety. Narrow
the bed we lie in, ample, our need.

Hunger waits with time on its side

LENINGRAD

I've heard stories about hunger:
my mother begging for turnips for two years,
my father roasting the tongues
of his boots when the war ended.
But neither had it as bad as the people
in Leningrad, sieged for nine-hundred days, three winters
without food. They traded diamond rings
and icons for meat patties. Human meat,
slightly sweet like horseflesh, though fattier.
I know it's easy to lose one's hunger:
after days, it deepens to a dull ache,
and after weeks of eating nothing,
the body's used itself
for fuel, and food's foreign as plastic.
But when instead of fasting you eat a little,
you remain ravenous, conscious
of sour breath and the stomach as an open sore,
and eager to admit that everything feeds
on something in this world.
For that admission, nothing expiates, not
the weekly air lift, not
parks lined by avenues of birches, not
voices in candlelit chapels,
and not summers
bathed in long, milky, northern light.

SUDANESE GIRL

(*TIME,* April 5, 1993, Pulitzer prize-
winning photo by Kevin Carter who
committed suicide July 27, 1994)

A vulture stands in rubble,
slivers of dried grass,
its legs grey stalks,
neck naked and bunched
between bony shoulders.

A child squats, too weak
to reach the feeding station,
head bowed to cracked clay,
skin loose on spiked bones,
black body a dusty grey,
only garment a neck-charm.

The horror of life feeding
on death spirals in my mind.
The child falters, falls,
forehead resting upon
a mound of parched earth.

I show the picture to my children.
My son-in-law recoils, his black
body velvet as a prancing pony's.
"Put the picture away," he says.
"Let's listen to music."

SCARCITY

I switch on the tube and see a land
where the span of scarcity is in direct
proportion to the avarice of its soul
that created a country with laws alien
to the most unmerciful of Gods. Bands
of youths, armed by warlords,
roam cities and countryside, like
death-knowing vultures circling in the sky,
ready to strike dead men and animals
which begin to swell, color of flies
and misery under a malign sun
breaking the earth's rhinoceros skin.

Ears of corn are fortuitous in the fields,
the grass once dependent on grace
or chance of winds and rains knows now
how ephemeral they are. The landscape
in tatters, has been forced to forgo its
habitual dole of sparse rains, few wells
and sparing pastures. The voice of water has
turned into clicks of pebbles, cracks of split
rocks, swish of dust blown by the South wind.
I know about hunger minimally and only
from the tube, which I cowardly switch off
at the shot of a starving baby so not to hear
                          his sinking cry.

BIRDMAN, SPRINGFIELD HOSPITAL

The sea gulls shift their wings,
cocked eyes pulp-tight,
and try to glide between
the thick folds of wind as
they sight the bread and
tunnel in, plucking the
soft dough from his broken fingers.

They smell his arrival every late
afternoon, when the burnt sun
is hidden behind the Solomon House,
when the other patients stagger on
the porch, some laughing,
some mute, some frightened at
the sudden spread of grey wings.

He ignores the faces on the porch,
their dry eyes, chattering teeth,
stopped throats, and clamps down the
marble steps to the open gazebo
where he sets the plastic
bag down and ceremoniously
begins to break the bread.

The birds circle and swoop,
an enormous rice paper origami,
smelling the crusts, sensing the torn
bites falling beneath his hand.
A man on the porch becomes anxious,
sputtering from behind his nervous beard,
he lifts his grey sleeves in flight.

They stare from behind the white
banisters, an assembly of dull points.
They watch the muscled dives,
lead wings dripping like storms,
the birds rising together and
then falling, curved and powerful,
calling out to their mark.

The birds hover high above the
gazebo as he picks up the empty bag
and heads back inside.
The patients move out of his way,
their heads down, silent,
their eyes as dark as a hooded falcon
who has just returned from the hunt.

POTATO PEELS

were given by
doctor's prescription
hefore starvation
people walked
with sunken black
or grey cheeks
glaring eyes
dragging along
like a cursed ghost
driven into court
yards where
garbage is piled
for a piece of potato
that can still
be licked a
rag that once
wrapped food
and can still
be gnawed at,
live out their
last days up
to their necks
in garbage

WILL WORK FOR FOOD

*Sign held by man at the corner of Manor
and Sweet Air*

Was it a steak dinner you were thinking of
when your bristly hand
borrowed the marker from
Starting Gate Hardware and
scratched in the capital letters?

Were you led by the smell of tomatoes
to this corner
to plant your feet
and smile
at the room mothers driving by?

Did you think you would be needed,
for housework
for babysitting
welcomed at the kitchen table
as they passed you the rolls?

Would the dry land
of the Air's old house
make you stand out among the dead ground,
your dress slacks
creased like corn husks?

Maybe the pastor's wife
would pull over

and have her young son
pour apples
into your hands.

Did you think
the people passing by,
their Mercedes racing
ahead of themselves,
would stop?

INSTANTÁNEA

No huele a flores la Plaza
de las Palomas, huele a vino,
a latas de cerveza.
Si andás desprevenido te sorprende
el tufo desparejo
de la miseria.

Al borde de la tarde
el camión de la sopa organiza
una fila obediente y resignada.
Este es el corazón
del barrio latino en Adams Morgan.

Apenas a unas cuadras
está la Casa Blanca.

SNAPSHOT

It doesn't smell like a plaza full of flowers.
Pigeon Park smells of wine,
beer cans.
If you just happen to be walking by there,
the squalid stench of misery
hits you.

On the edge of dusk
the soup truck organizes
an obedient and resigned line.
This is the heart
of the *barrio* in Adams Morgan.

Just a few blocks away
is the White House.

MEDELENA

All the children that came out of me
are still alive. I did it.

Sister Gracia calls their father
my husband. For seven years
I lived where he had me,
an abandoned ranch full of magic and spiders.

One noon he told Mama he was taking me to mass.
I was 14. I pulled up my socks.
I'd never been inside a haunted house.
I knew a man could push his muscle
into you, I understood it, the world
splitting clean down the middle;
I saw stars slide through the jagged glass
still in the frames, heard rats chewing.
Later, his feet curled into mine, sleeping,
and it wasn't so awful. I laughed at the priest,
his tight jaw when he told me I should go back
to my mother's shawls, my father's Sunday beatings.

My man came on Sundays through the broken window,
bringing me a melon or a box of crackers.
I sat on a corner in Durango: three crates,
parcels of peanuts, those flat white packages
of marzipan stamped with roses,
M & Ms. Lined up against the wall,
Vidaluz, Pablo, Carlos, Juancito.
All the children that came out of me.

One Sunday his fist fell so hard I couldn't
see the children. It was only the cane rum
that did it, but I knew I had to leave.

That's when I fought my road war, keeping
Juancito breathing, Carlos from cramming
bugs in his mouth. I joked with my babies,
stroking their elbows so they wouldn't understand
the name the beggars called me, spitting.
Pablo's job was claiming the abandoned
shed near the dump of every village.

I nursed my four-year-old. I called Vidaluz
sister to have someone to talk to.
We crawled north, the snake with ten legs
that coughed all night.

In Juarez my cousin watched the children
and they stopped laughing. When I was fired
I found them locked in her closet.

That's over. Everything's over, even
crossing the river in inner tubes, losing
Juancito's blanket. I found walls with ivy.
The Sisters took me in. I do laundry.
I live in the little house behind the priest's.
In the evenings I sit on the porch and watch
my children get fatter, take life in their teeth.
The Sisters gave a party when I turncd 23;
a used coat and winter hats for the children.

The only magic left is what I see
in the blankness beyond the glass at night:
My hands stubbornly peeling Carlos' fingers
from the inner tube (watch him swirl down with the blanket),
Pablo's skull wrapped with the fancy
marzipan in the market, Vidaluz'
head tipped back. No fear. One stroke.
The hand behind the glass shard,
mine.

I HAVE HUNGERED FOR THE FLAT GOLD

I have hungered for the flat gold of your foot.
I have known myself indulgent, shivering
at the press of curved palm against flesh
that is planed, a breathing metal plate
yielding sharp current. It is the alien
quality of your heat that drives and grounds me.
Your body is a shadowless bronze desert.
Your coppery eyelid knows no fold.

WHAT IS A POEM? WHAT IS HOME?

*after Lorraine Ndlovu's interviews
with children*

Christinah Somo—health: eyes good.
Headache sometimes. Once treated for TB.
She hears and understands but she forgets
things. Even when sent to the store for food.

No time to study. No time
to learn. Even in the heat
she aches with cold. Mother
father drink and fight. Sweat.

Sello Mashiane—he stays with relatives. Sometimes
he visits home but the parents are away to sell
the *baas's* eggs. He sleeps on the floor.
The dung is warm and the hair mites are gone.

Flaubert visited Paris
and hated humanity. Here
there's the story of the father
who steals the money saved
for the children's milk.

September summer is coming.
Does anyone hear the thunder
or does it travel past
like a shadow
without greeting?

LISTENING FOR WINGS

Lately, I forget
about watering the bromeliad,
my old refrigerator
groans under a glacier,
the gutters are stuffed
and I think
something is living
in the sofa cushions
on the porch.

At work
all the talk is flimsy as tissue,
a feverish wind
wails down the hall,
I pry at a window
but paint seals it shut,
and I find on my desk
a calendar
with half the days missing.

Terrible
to be neither myself
nor a part of anything larger,
full of unreal wishes,
listening for wings
or the opening of the door to the sea,
as if
something has shoved me
outside of my life.

And last night
in my dream
an Etruscan soothsayer,
a haruspex,
poked my entrails
with a stick,
and predicted
from my shrivelled and ravaged liver
the end of civilization.

WINTER, 1933, OHIO

We had ham,
grape jam.
Where'd she scrounge
the sugar?
She, the ghost
in all machines?
We ate.

No heat
no coal
except for a hearth
that melted
milk in saucepans.
Bellies baked,
Backsides cold,
We ate.

Born a farmer,
He drummed oil
house to house;
Held out samples
green and amber
in glass tubes.

Gasman came,
Unscrewed the meter.
She sped, honked the horn,
shrieked "I can't cook...
You must not..." Humbled,
cringing, we ate.

Fellow farmers,
as dead broke as he,
liked him, wearing
charm on his sleeve.
We ate.

Will the Bitter,
like some forms of madness,
one day fade away?
Devoid of hope,
hung with rags,
Sick and blind
as old Jerusalem,
We ate.

FORM AND CONTENT

The woman I met
in a downtown park
sitting beside a bed
of white chrysanthemums
told me her birthday
falls early in June,
on the same day as mine.

She also said
schizophrenics improve
if kept in trapezoidal wards.
I admitted that statistics
and abstractions both bore me.
But mirrors angled in windows
to show who's walking up the street,
or quartets with only three players
interest me.

She mentioned universals:
spirals in turrets of mollusks.
concentric rings in trees,
the recognition scene implied in every dream.

None of the nights of love are the same,
I told her.
And memories may turn to wolves,
legends to quarantines,
drops of ink to mirrors of the past.

Yet she insisted on first principles:
lines alternating on a zebra's back,

grids in a honeycomb,
the pattern of an updraft of air.

Each as inevitable as our meeting tomorrow
beside our bed of white chrysanthemums—
You'll come, won't you, she said.
And I saw I was in over my head.

TIME ON ITS SIDE

Hunger crawls in a crooked line,
Hunger stalks from here, to there, to nowhere.
Hunger speaks in small mouths of rice.
Hunger counts backwards like a patient anesthetized.

Hunger growls regardless of its leash.
Hunger is a straw-empty cage of lies.
The lens of its stare ready to ignite,
Hunger sprawls patiently in the sun.

Hunger knows its whims, is terminal.
Hunger never asks, "Am I my brother's keeper?"
Hunger is sloppy, skin-taut and navel protruded
like a series of ellipses.

Hunger breaks no bones.
Hunger, nothing less than a corpse's other masque,
Is visible, lonely,
Consecrated with flies that hover like dirt angels

Praying over their victims.
And here no lilies smolder at the edges,
Putting on airs—
Hunger waits with time on its side.

BECAUSE OF THE STARVING

It begins when you're made
to clean up your plate because
people are starving in— fill in
the blank. For me, it was India.

From then on, you're haunted.
Gaunt possibilities squat on
emaciated legs; dark eyes
stare at those grains of rice

you are wasting. Their village
stands in perpetual drought: land's
parcelled out so no irrigation schemes
work. The women do double work

in the fields, in their families,
yet find time to paint. Their walls
picture Rama's wife Sita carried off
by the demon Ravanna in a palanquin

or today's bride, after puberty, being
carried to her husband's village
in a palanquin, painted by Sita Devi,
married off at age twelve

to a poor Brahmin priest, four
daughters dying in childhood,
too undernourished (as girls often
are) to fight off the cholera.

In despair, their mother turns to
the powerful Durga, Mother
Goddess, and recites her a poem-
prayer daily, and paints

the way she once painted on her
arms, her school slate, on the ground:
then was punished for wasting time.
During the 1968 famine

in Bihar, she's 'discovered.'
When she exhibits in Delhi
will Durga protect her
so no one will cut off

her hands out of spite?
Her son comes with her to D.C.,
eats ice cream with every meal,
even breakfast—just like

my husband when he first came
from India. I'd rather
talk philosophy, religion,
ideas, but reality

intrudes. When I'm in India
I cover my plate with my hands,
rudely refusing what I might
waste—because of the starving.

INTERVAL

We know
it is only a matter of time
before the distance
collapses in on us,
before we feel
the fur of the world:

              a train
bearing its cargo
of hands
holding our ankles down
while we strain
with our necks
for air

or an innocent helicopter
calmly patrolling
the river, brother
to the ones that carry
the wounded
back from the north,
the sky filled up
with their insect shapes.

             The feet
of the hanged ones
swing over our heads like
brass censers
from their chains.
Our frightened god flies
like a bat
through his cave.

At dawn
a horn will sound;

we dance on
numbed by a music
no revolution has prepared
while out on the floor
of the desert hunger
offers its breast.

Raw
chords
ready for
song

THE CHINESE INSOMNIACS

It is good to know
the Chinese insomniacs.
How, in 495 A.D.,
in 500 B.C.,
the moon shining, and the pine-
trees shining back
at it, a poet had to walk
to the window.

It is companionable
to remember my fellow
who was unable to sleep
because of a sorrow, or not;
who had to watch
for the wind
to stir night flowers in the garden
instead of making the deep journey.

They live nine hun-
dred years apart,
and turn, and turn, restless.
She says her sleeve is wet
with tears; he says something difficult ·
to forget, like
music counts the heartbeat.

A date is only a mark
on paper—it has little to do
with what is long.
It is good to have their company
tonight: a lady, awake
until birdsong;
a gentleman who made
poems later out of frag-
ments of the dark.

TELL ME COLOR

School taught blue, taught
yellow, red; primary
mixes: purple, green.
Pink, a concession,
a watering down.

But you said lapis, pumpkin,
ocher, delphinium.
Light was a ladder
of changes
you taught me to climb:

sand, ash, mahogany,
cinnamon. Quick as
they shift, you
were quicker, took
each on a flick

of your lizard-quick
tongue tasting
apricot, raspberry, wine.
School taught number.
I was five.

Your pied skirts
draped in fadeless
confidence, you
called out names
from the rosters of light.

THE MOON ON HER BIRTHDAY

Tonight the moon has put her sisters
to bed early
and has taken her oboe down
to the stream

If she wanted to play all the old
songs she knows by heart
she might pick a spot
under the familiar willow
but tonight she wants to describe
how the water knows
her footsteps though she herself
does not know the water

So she goes over to where
the farmer's fence comes down
through the last of the hills
and the field ends
and there sits on a rock above the water
with the oboe beside her
and remembers the farmer's wife
holding out her hands for the very things
she knows she will never have

But just *how* she comes to
this woman's dream and desire
and how she comes to see
her own face in the tiny pools of water
left by the hooves of the horses in the mud
is exactly the mystery
waiting and the dark and the music

will solve   the kind of music
that is moonlight
the farmer's wife will wake to
puzzled but happy
in the middle of the night

NOW IS THE TIME OF NOSTALGIA

Take big Bessie Smith, loving
to sing the country of her varicose veins
or Georgia O'Keeffe's bones
on the chalky desert wall. The burst
of a dark orchid: Piaf!
Piaf! they would cry
and *The Blue Angel* still plays.

Abbey Lincoln moans. Somewhere
the *chansons* of Brel are belted,
lilted, and luring in rows
of smoky rooms where people lived
with terror, the edge
the other side
of beauty.

And a blackberry
wide-eyed woman child dreams
after school
in the local public library.
She meets a faded photograph
—some Josephine Baker, a gramophone
exotic tongue. She sees

the bronze flesh dancing, a stranger,
some kind of
mother.
She walks now unseen,
homeward, to her brothers
and supper of yellow corn,
sugared beans.

THE MUSE CHECKED OUT LAST WEEK

She left nouns in my belly,
verbs stacked in my throat,
puffy and sore,
some non-medicine,
scatter of sleep.
Dreams disappear
before memory can swallow,
bitter or not,
shoot back
into blood,
make them breathe.
I want poems
about hands,
bones, hair,
but nothing hums,
gets struck by the eye
of first light.
I can't find the raw chord
ready for song,
the breath-word-breath
like foot pounding pavement,
street after street,
every smell
a different life,
cedar, rain,
a sauce from Afghanistan.
When slick wood speaks
through the bottoms
of my feet,

and a single moment
is prayer.
Some mute skin stretches
over thin lines
as they coil,
beg her tongue
to come alive again.

CICADAS

may it not rather be that he wrote it,
wrote a Word so long we have yet to come
to the end of it?

J. M. Coetzee

No act of God, this blank scrap
glaring angrily up Sunday morning
in cicada June. For 17 silent years
whirring welled underground. Now
it cuts across the grain of summer
with the sound of a circular saw.

For weeks I have longed to rise up
pen in hand, and see, smell, feel
sawdust flying, the breasts
of poets beating:

Keep it coming, keep it going,
keep it coming, keep it going.

THE FAILING

Before that, I believed I saw things very clearly,
I had a sort of intimacy with the whole, with the universe.
Then suddenly it became alien. You are yourself;
and the universe is beyond, which is altogether incomprehensible.
—*Alberto Giacometti*

That day dawned like any other: violet
washed into rose and flowed into ribbons
of softest pink. The sun crept up,
a diffident burst of amarillo,
and the sparrows let fly a wild hurrah.
I remember leaves the color of young
pears, that broad, cool spatula
taking its ease, and the first touch
of clay tucked under dampened cloth.
Another day loving the shapes of things!
I splashed water on my face, opened my eyes,
and—just like that—my world had disappeared.
Leaves, birds, sun, sky driven so far back
my gaze failed to reach them. Failed and failed.

That was years ago. I still live in this space
as white and vast as time. I move my brush—
space swallows it whole. I erect a palace
of wire and string; by 4 a.m. the thing
is down to its frail bones while the spine hangs
in a vanishing cage, and my eyes
become holes that filter nothing.
"Revise, revise," I mutter to my tortured bronze.
Diego sits like a lump of metal. He *is* metal.
I try again. I put him in a sweater.
Dawn comes and goes; again I fail;

then night arrives without the moon and stars.
Before sleep takes my tired eyes, I want
to see the coming day when I will

raise a small, unsteady sun and set this thin man
walking straight into the land that left me
empty, empty, empty. Perhaps the sun will shine.

GEORGE YATER'S SELF-PORTRAIT—1930

The eyes give him away
his lust
for the brightness beneath skin
the desperate wanting
of a lover being summoned
indifferent
to the light-starved world
He stalks his prey

He is ready to die
for that lissome muse
who demands always
just a little more
And he'd devour her
if she'd let him
They both know this
So she waits
just out of reach

Her breath caresses
his long-ago skin
Her shadow blossoms
on his mirrored flesh
His eye traces the curve
of her body
She calls him out
He goes for the kill
that blood-filled, glistening moment
when flesh becomes light

WOMAN SINGING

The trees can smell us.
They like how we smell when we are unsure—
    that heat of violet verging on rose.

And porch boards
    stay firm under the sudden imbalance of night.

Though not one kiss has been stolen the sirens wail.

No honey without the tongue, no crystal without the sword:
voice, love, with which I am cowardly nightly and full of bees.

Voice that says
    my jewel is clover between your lips
    and the dead are larger than airplanes.

    (This diamond voice, cut from earth,
takes great delight in reminding me.)

That trees can smell us.
They change their minds and plunge like horses
    touched with an unsure hand:
    ice, large, metal, ink.

And porch boards
    sink under the weight of the unexploded.

    *

The record is old and the song older.
She left her father's house, it says,
to marry an outlawed man.
    (This was the Highlands. Outlawed men
    were common as crows
    and as clannish.) He's dead, she sings,
    and I marry him, Father, a thousand times more in your eye.

In some versions, the child is cut from her womb by the sword that kills her.
In some she dies in snow.

Neither death stops her singing, and no
      arrangement of verses stops the singing of hounds.

Hunted with dogs—did I forget that part?
But never mind. Four hundred years pass
      in the silent groove after her singing.

And in the New World only the trees can smell us.

           *

Four hundred years—
         and still she is sure
that crows fly from your hair to my small hours.

Everything rising. The porch is too low but the voice won't climb.

Everything rising and how will I know—I won't know—
      the full moment until it begins to recede.

           *

In some versions I have the courage of trees,
      in some the wings of kisses.
I give you up, I throw you down, I snow.
In some versions you are cut from me by the diamond voice of sirens.

But nothing stops the singing.

     It flowers in rock, cleaves like scent
       till a thousand bees

hound me into fracture, into rose.

           *

Which nothing stops from singing.

COMUNICACIÓN

Yo te hablo de poesía
y vos me preguntás
a qué hora comemos.
Lo peor es que
yo también tengo hambre.

COMMUNICATION

I am talking to you about poetry
and you say
when do we eat.
The worst of it is
I'm hungry too.

SONG FOR MY LADY, OR EXCUSE ME McCOY

i am tired of women who love musicians
who desire to be loved by musicians
who think that musicians are the best lovers
and the best players
i am tired
and do not care to listen to this anymore
do not sing to me or hum to me
or proclaim to me a new music
there is NO music
coltrane is dead
parker is dead
navarro is dead
young is dead
cannonball has just died and
so have herbie sanders and benson
and i don't even listen to radio
i am so tired
of women sitting in clubs
sipping drinks of coke and rum
pretending to be billie bessie betty or whomever
laying around between acts
being very hip
i am very tired
of the woman who tells me that the man
she loves is in europe
back from europe
or heading for europe
i am tired of music lovers

coming down from new york
telling me about the apple
if you are william tell please do not take aim at my head
i am tired and need no second headaches
i do not need another woman to tell me
that what's hers belongs to the drummer
and what's mine is fine
but it just don't swing
i am tired of telling women
that i am better than bebop
that what i got is the new thing
that i can play an instrument as good as anyone
i am tired of telling them this
so from now on
whenever i hear a woman
talking about some musician
about how way-out his sound is
about how his music gets all up inside and moves her around
from now on when i hear a woman talking about a musician
i'm gonna turn my back like miles
pull my hat down like monk
disappear like rollins
and maybe come back next year
if i feel like it and if she's ready

ONE OF THE REASONS

The street is
a cathedral, even better
because the storefronts' brick
vaulting returns
my eye to earth. While the lame
girl's lame leg's
fluttering
her blue skirt, her mother
yanks her hand, says
Come on
which is not so bad as it might sound and is
maybe a kind of prayer, after all: irregular
gait & words, they
walk that way, don't
get me wrong. There are

lots of junk stores open. Floating
on the lake of a blue-mirrored
Art Deco table, a wicker bait basket
overflows with lures: little radiant
fish; metallic lights
barbed with hooks, who would not
want to eat you? I am so easily
convinced by things—by *things*, I mean—
I am fluttering, a blue skirt
ruffling like a lake. Rhythm
means fr. *rhein* to flow—more
at *stream.* Imagine

how many things there are to buy and imagine
you would never get tired of buying them—
not just the antherium in the slender Steuben vase
but also house slippers, bok choy, fleshy pink
bunion pads, linguine, Sardo, birds'
shadows on sidewalks, the whole
painted-over storefront
of the Holiness Pentecostal Church.

This is just
one of the reasons
I like
certain poems, the old lady
right now perilously
crossing the street
against traffic, the weighted
left pocket of her
unseasonable cloth coat
against which the rich
secret
of her handbag
strikes.

WHY WE DO THIS

after seeing the Martin Puryear exhibit
at the Hirshhorn

We wrap ourselves in wood, smooth strips of sapling,
the bark peeled back, vine bent and soaked
of resistance. Woven wooden strips form cages
to hold us. Our bodies are cages. Our bodies are covered
with wood, light seeps in if we let it.   Our bodies gleam
in light, small as we are, small in the darkness.

                                      We turn in the darkness.
Wooden spokes of wooden wheels. In cages, our bodies turn.
We want the turning. In darkness, the turning is all
we want, the friction of motion, the movement of wood turning
toward smoothness, the body caught, for a moment, suspended
and open, the thin slits of light shining through.

CAVE PAINTER

Resurrecting the fire, his second hunt begins.
He wakes tired, retelling this life,
trailing little spots of blood to mark
the dawn, kneeling by the huge patches
he finds, red and luminous at night.
Hungering, he pantomimes for days,
stroking his way through faint snow
again, following the sound, pushing ahead
to where the junipers buried it.
Dragging a sled of branches back,
he remembers the head and antlers wobbling,
feels the weight of his arms once more.
Always the eyes stare back from his story.
When a low moan begins, far from the firelight
dying, the cave's ceiling and floor fade
to a dim crawlspace. Like the wind
it can be forgotten. He learns to sleep
beside this sound, grinning the good
dream that tickles, sobbing
into his reddish hands.

HOW HIGH THE MOON

I dreamt Virgil Waggoner
again last night
trying to kill himself with a trombone.
Fat Virgil
grey as an oyster—
all he had was blowing
and they told him it would
blow him away
but when the sweat
and the booze and smoke
under silver spots
burn your eyes
your breath and your beat
become the swinging
and you blow, man
you chop into that syncopated fluid
and your ax is
the glistening link between
the galaxies
and nothing matters—
not love
nor light
and sound is light
and light is blowing
and the beat is
your crippled heart
and dead is maybe
    blowing across the galaxies.

DEEP INSIDE DANNY
BUT STILL VISIBLE BEHIND THE GLASSES

Hey!
I can play piano louder,
    better, wilder, madder
than anyone on this Beach!

I can play stride
two handed
like James P. Johnson and
    Fats Waller
only faster on the runs
faster than Peterson
faster than Tatum—
I wear dark glasses
because my fingers
hurt my eyes.

Hey!
I can thump like Garner
and pump like King Cole and
    Teddy Wilson put together,
I can blow Mozart behind my back
and Scriabin in my sleep
and rags and bop
like Eubie and Monk,

and when I sit down
with a drummer and bass
I can grab a chord and rattle it
like Beethoven bones in a soup can.

MANSON MASSACRE

I'm taking part in a movie about a Manson type massacre. People randomly get their bodies slashed with razorblades or hacked with an ax while trying to eat a plate of scrambled eggs. One guy with an ax sticking to the back of his head keeps dripping blood on his plate. I go on watching, hoping the heroine kills everybody and runs away with the money but I have to run outside to the parking lot and throw up. Meanwhile a lot of people are walking into the next performance, laughing and telling me "He who throws up first is the guilty one."

after frank o'hara

what little wind there is
swells the shades
i will mark with a skull and crossbones
before sailing across tributaries roaring
at the ancient t-shirt
i have turned into a bandana

the ends of which undulate like pigtails
and the waves which threaten to steal
pillows already moist with rainwater,
anxious to reach the brownstone where you are

How
embrace
my
nakedness

LOOKING AT MEN

Yesterday, a man asked me
why I was traveling alone.
If he were my husband,
he would not permit me to
go away. It says in the
Koran the woman is the
comfort of the man's
body.   *   The men took
turns picking leeches off
each other's bodies. When
the war ended, the smell
of fresh soap made them
vomit.   *   A man and his
son and a horse. The father
says: Get up on the horse.
As they journey they pass
a jeering crowd. How can
you let your old father walk
while you ride? they ask
the boy. The father climbs
up behind his son and they
continue on their journey.
They pass a group of people
working in a field. How can
you both ride, wearing out
your old horse? they ask.
In the end the father and
son carry the horse.   *
I watch a man quicken as he
crosses a mine field, as he
climbs into a bunker and
takes up his submachine
gun.   *   Replacements

have come for instruction.
The sergeant picks up a
smooth metal ring. Do you
know, he looks into their
boys' faces, what these
can do?   *   Beneath me
a man's head is the only
marker as he walks the
labyrinth of trenches: this
one's never seen war. He
feels the earth around his
body, the closest he's come
to his own grave.   *   At
night a man smokes a
cigarette when he cannot
sleep. These are true
stories of a personal nature.
*   From letters I know
how a man wishes to be seen.
From sleeping with him I know
how a man is.   *   Under
me a man holds perfectly
still to see how long he can
stay inside me without
coming.   *   A man, partly
blind, touches my back lightly
with one finger to learn
where he is in this world.
I mistake it for love.   *
Lady, a man calls to me,
beautiful lady, if only you
knew what you wanted, I would
show it to you.

BRAIN CHEMISTRY

In the dark,
we are victim.
The attack can come
from behind, vicious
with a blunt weapon or
in the slow spin
of a car into oncoming traffic.

There is a curtain,
a certain fog where
we become the secret
alchemist, translator
of codes that station amnesia,
obsession as guards around
those cranial horizons.

COURSES

I flinch as
the needle searches
across my hand,
once,
twice,
in at last.
The relief is short-lived
as the fire surges up my arm,
leaping from bone to bone
over the underbrush of cells.
I become the hardness of my skull
beneath taut skin.
Inch-by-inch every pore draws out its tears
until the heat dims.

Tomorrow will awaken me
with that morning slap of nausea.
It will be no early and accustomed sign
of nurture, flesh of my flesh,
but a stranger tracking
through my veins, search-
and-destroy chemistry:
the caustic midwife of my future.

I must learn
to love this fire,
bless each translucent drop
and know some sacrament of grace
among the IV's and the alcohol.
I pray.
I long for the heaven
of a half-century
and my children grown.

DELIVERANCE

To swaddle a struggling toddler
facing a painful procedure
you use the papoose board.
Four strips of canvas
fastened with Velcro
fix arms and legs and head
to a mummy-shaped slab.

Little Jose, at thirteen months
too strong to be held,
lies on the board
one arm extended.
Terrified, he throws his head
side to side,
screams.

Above him his mother
hovers, an engine
of instinct.
In one fluid move
she lets down her full breast,
massive, warm
the color of earth.

It covers his face,
is all he can see
all he has to hold on to.
His open mouth roots around wildly,
fills with the nipple
latches on,
sucks.

THE PROMISE

If you could just lose weight
your blood pressure would go down
your diabetes would clear up
you could get off all those pills you take
your joints wouldn't ache
you could climb the stairs
run after the bus
carry the groceries
pick up the baby
the swelling in your legs would go down
you could reach all the way to your aching feet
you could breathe again

You could find clothes to fit
get out of your slippers and into real shoes
who knows but what your old man would come back
you'd get more respect from your children
a decent job
your son would kick drugs
your daughter wouldn't get pregnant again
you'd live to see your last one grown

Your neighbors wouldn't talk about you
the toilet would flush
the roof wouldn't leak
there'd be food enough at the end of the month
they wouldn't cut off your check
jack up the rent
you'd hit the number
go off for two weeks in Aruba

Jesus would save the world from sin
those who mourn would be comforted
the poor would enter the Kingdom of God
your hunger would be filled.

THIGMOTAXIS*

Call it an embrace,
each poem,
an uncontrollable leaning,
my sending them to you.
Take it as positive,
the gesture is toward,

unavoidable, our alignment in space.
Call it habit, the emptiness
a starling embraces
as she opens her beak, lunges toward
nothing—
I turn to you, perhaps

a response could brace
the poem,
keep it from waiting
for maternal promise to lean
against its hungry mouth,
that soft space

of need.
Call it a conversation, a space
leading us toward
an affirmable silence,
like the quickening a woman feels
when the unborn turns.

Call it an act—
the captive hummingbird fastening
shadows to a twig.
Remembering her nest
she weaves space and embraces
the memory of embrace.

*An organism's drive to press up against its parent

THE JELLO MAN ON THE FEAST
OF CIRCUMCISION

(Feeding Program, St. Stephen of
the Incarnation, Washington, D.C.)

The mendicants shuffle by, accepting, sullen,
Their eyes unable to focus on servers
Whose food, like smelling salts, accentuate
The pain. At the end of the long New Year line
I am the jello man, the jello man,
Slopping generous portions of free church food
With my practiced, institutional scoop.
The necks that gulp like starving chickens
Have slits in them, thin as switchblades
Direct to a vein, yesterdays'
Precise cuttings to the bone.

FOR MY FIRST GRADE TEACHER
AND HER SPECIAL MESSENGER

I thought you were without genitals, that nothing cracked you
    open and made you insatiable.
I thought the blood ran clear out of you like out of the side of
    Christ.
I thought your whole body was made of chalk dust, flaking ash.
Without children, your body burning in a yellow godlight.
Your brain, a seamless garment buried beneath your eyes.

Maybe it was God who taught you cruelty—
the black boy you made sit in his shit until it dried
had to stand up and say pardon me sister pardon me class
for the rest of eternity.

You could make a child stutter at her book.
You could make a child recognize his rot.
Perhaps you did it by ignoring, by letting be what had already
    happened.
A girl carried your words on paper,
walking past the huge stone statues.

What was she but a poor Irish factory worker's daughter
disappearing inside
the harrowing cleanliness and bright light?

A HOUSE IS A STORY

To begin, there is a room
so full of people it takes you
most of your life to enter.
For years you didn't try, only peering
sideways through the locked glass doors.
There is your breath, soft on the pane.
You pause, try to change, or shed the invisible
face of your inheritance. You reach
for any hand to carry you in.
When someone finally shrugs and steps aside,
you slip by with your eyes down—
one of the tasks agreed on
silently when they built this house
against the rain, against a voice
rising inside, making room.

MISSING SLEEP

Slow down
sleep is not
the kind of train
you can run for,

remember
a crossing of tracks
with sand and still water
far back.

all your missed trains
set out
the steam and little bells
look for you

the wails and swinging
lights go out
to find you
at the old secret,

that foggy swamp
where there's
a rowboat
a boy you know

and ticking rails
half a mile short
of the boarded-up
hometown station.

CHRYSANTHEMUMS

I have called into service
my powerful nose, a nose to rival
Cyrano's, since mine is tapered and bulbous
at once—a haughty Jew's nose
which in its youth aspired to prodigy.

With it I sniff your warmer left wrist,
the one nearest the heart, in this way
recounting the numberless nights I have
put on your scent, that zany excretion of kin
and want, a bear among chrysanthemums.

THE GYM

You saw that picture of me with a flat belly,
a tilt to my chin and a neckness to my neck.
They call what happened to me letting yourself go.
Where is it I went? To the couch. To the movies.
To anything sweet such as recklessness. What
followed? Enormous t-shirt dresses. My daughter's
arguments. My husband's forgetfulness. I just got
back from my own remembering. They call what I'm doing

now, getting a hold of yourself. For this in the gym
there is a machine, clever as a flush toilet.
It comes in chrome and leatherette with no opinions
or judgments, just waiting for me, the essential
moving part. I lie on my back testing the weight
in an attitude practiced in love and birth
but this time I rock by myself, back and forth.

REBECCA

will i hate mirrors?
will i hate reflections?
will i hate to dress?
will i hate to undress?

jim my husband
tells me it won't matter
if i have one or two
two or one it doesn't matter
he says

but it does
i know it does

this is my body
this is not south africa or nicaragua
this is my body
losing a war against cancer
and there are no demonstrators outside
the hospital to scream stop

there is only jim
sitting in the lobby
wondering what to say
the next time we love
and his hands move towards
my one surviving breast

how do we convince ourselves
it doesn't matter?
how do i embrace my own nakedness
now that it is no longer complete?

WANT

In the cold house she revels in denying warmth. So spare
she can hear her own bones climb stairs, her cheeks sinking further.
What she parcels out she knows piece by piece: two linen napkins,
a pair of polished forks. Half glasses of wine. Several heels of bread
which collect themselves from various meals: last week's pale roast,
one night with company. She's always wanting. That way she can say
she is alive. Famine entices her, the need for touch, the lack of excess
like a cotton dress she wears to church. Her father taught her how to stave
off full, how to empty pockets, live on next to nothing. When the nuns
pressed her for quarters, she stared them down till they moved
to someone generous. She learned to love her ribs, facts which proved
her abstinence. Even now she takes him only when the pain greatens after
months, his pleas behind her, her enormous want begging to be fed.

FOOD, CLOUDS, & SECRETS

1. A Distance

Season of possibility.
Azaleas, spilling out of themselves,
the dense mist of apple blossoms.
The world re-opens with a gush
like newly-tooled valves
in an old heart. From the bright meadow,
the girl studies the underbellies of clouds
with the acute attention
of the deprived.

*

Always, the issue was food.
Though her mother would cook favorite meals
to tempt her—roast beef and yorkshire pudding,
or fettucine, or leg of lamb—
she'd sit before the Wedgewood and crystal
and multiple silver settings, arranging
and rearranging the food on her plate.
She'd glance at her parents,
as they'd slice the meat
and bring the food so carefully to their mouths
with left hands, tines of forks downturned,
as the English do.

*

Each day she'd stand before the usual mirror
like an obsessed scientist
at her microscope,
always too much to see,
too small a field of view.

*

When she could not get out of bed
the doctor was summoned,
and the scale that recorded her 100 pounds,
which meant she had finally achieved
what she was after.
She ate enough to work the cider press
that afternoon, to compete with a flurry of armed bees,
that hovered and buzzed over mashed fruits.
While around her,
apples fell and rattled in the dry leaves.

*

Then, the change—
she could not eat enough,
yet everything she ate sickened her.
She'd stand at the sink, suds to her elbows,
and with her mother's back turned,
pick left-overs off plates and pop them in her mouth
before the dish disappeared beneath the water.
She'd clean up after herself
in the bathroom and kitchen, though she could not materialize
the missing volumes of food. No words were exchanged,
and yet her mother knew.
From then on, her mother knew,
which was, after all, what she wanted, really:
an unshared common secret.
From her room, wretched with forced emptiness,
she'd watch flocks of starlings
populate the opaque sky,
her throat abraded from the ravages
of fingernails.

*

How are we worthy
of anyone's love?
How do we know when we've taken enough?
How do we know what to give when nothing suffices?
How do we make our mothers
want to be our mothers?
How do we take what we need and no more?

2. Toward the Mother

This morning, I walked into the garden.
The dry earth buckled
around the tomato plants,
the sunflowers stood runted,
their heads bowed, eclipsing nothing.
I am beginning to understand
that forgiveness comes on its own, like rain,
revealing and consoling at the same time,
a softening in memory, a distance.

When sick as a child
I wanted you to sit
at the edge of my bed, to have
all the time in the world
as if your presence
were the only nourishment.

*We all have a private world
no one should be privy to*, you said,

I had my private world.
I had my secret.

Still, I wanted to give you
what I thought you wanted.
But I am not the son
my brothers never could be.
I am the food that you refuse to eat.
I am the fork in my own hand,
never clean enough.

*

Remember how, as a girl,
I would wait for thunderstorms
on our back porch?—
the distant rumble,
the metallic earthy scent
of forthcoming rain.
Even now, as I wait for what is imminent,
I envy the clouds
that purge themselves so gracefully
of what it is that makes them clouds.

soblack

see

I am not white

I do not aspire to be
white

I work hard to stay
black

bold/italic/black
incense oil
burning candle black

I want to
think black
love black
taste black
teach black
bitchblack
inkblack

I want to pitch
my voice midnight
drumout my name

say I've known rivers
instead of I pledge allegiance
sing god bless the chile
instead of america

I want to be rawblack

I want to be soblack
shacks grow out of my back
dandelion greens sprout
my eyes

I want to be bossblack
three-piece corporate image

nappy edges   grandbouba
briefcase   gutblack
gourmet
chitlin circuit
hamboneblack

I am a state of emergency

I want to be soblack
antjamimas n uncletoms

who say black black black
I'm sick of hearing it
loosen they bandanas when
they smell me coming

I want to be soblack
f b i taps my phone
cause they think I am
malcolm reincarnate

I want to be razorblack
get arrested for
slicin the moon into
three equal planets

ghetto
bantustan
reservation

I want to be screamingblack
so squad cars
screech to a halt when
I walk cross the street
I want to be sweet streetblack
so I am booked for
disturbing the peace

arrest me
arrest me

yes

I am a state of emergency

I am the
big butt
loud lip
loose hip
ret tittied
tambourine
shoutin
switchblade
cussin
aretha singin
lena lovin
momma

> *the*
> *boogie woogie*
> *rumble of a dream*
> *deferred**

arrest me
arrest me

I am the
oogha boogha
jungle bunny
voodoo mule
common
bare breasted
bare footed
dancing
licorice sweet

down
any street

I sing

I testify

I call

> Ago ou we
> attibon legba
> ouvri bayé pou moin
> ouvri bayé**

arrest me
arrest me

pleaze

* from Langston Hughes
** Vodun ceremonial song

Unexplained territories

EATING LONDON

He went to London, full of what he didn't have,
to see it all. He ate a couple tour books.
Michelin gave him indigestion. Fodor had
an aftertaste of fish and chips, two things
he hated together that he loved alone.
He ate them anyway, down to the last syllable
of the final signature. He ate the upper decks

off several buses, the 25, the 74
as it rolled along the Brompton Road.
He drank the Thames to the sea, he walked
his bones to their knees. Big Ben told some lies
he checked his watch against. The poets slept on
as the poets will. The Parliament sat and sat.
The pubs called time when the time was out.

The curtains rose, the curtains fell. He bit
between the lines, learned an appetite for what
was not. He ate his way through Shakespeare, ate
the paintings at the Tate, ate Drury Lane.
He fed himself up in London, then he came home
to diet on what he hadn't seen before, the places
where he thought he'd been, the fullness of the pause.

24, AVENUE DE LA BORNALA

Young in America I fished the Saugatuck
for nothing—an altarboy crowded
with tiny sins. Verdi crowds the room now
with shudders. I look to the clock,
the volet again.

I left that country on a north Jersey swamp
and turned by cabin pressure
above the black Atlantic,
till grey light said turning was done
over Ireland.

London slopped in mist before my eyes.
I emerged with one mind, two bags, and uneasy.
When I woke to Cambridge, a cold
lunged at me from mold under thatch.
And Dover sunk, a dream in fever,
under the sunless Channel.

More hot drizzle, then Dieppe, whose rooves
were borrowed from Boston. My country tugged
at me, sweet land, insisting fragments.

Without the word I lost the "gare," but found
the shifting Seine. Next night's fog train
was shared with an Italian, whose penknife
knew salami by heart. Around dawn, he told me
Toulon was St. Raphaël, and I said "grazie,"
and barely made it back on board
before the train pulled out.

No tiny swirls of dust and scraps of paper,
but Sunday morning pigeons milled about,
finally, the vacant taxi stand, finally,
about this country I'd travelled into.

Now schoolkids chase recess on the roof
across the street. And the rouget I fry
for lunch stinks burnt.

NIAGARA

We stood on the edge in the crowd
watching the gulls mount
the lit spray into soaking sun
as lovers rise on the heat of sex
through their own histories into ours
and we were, with everyone, with the water.
sunlit and shining and wet

but back home watching you sleep
I am still behind the rail
seeing the endless fall
of green current to gray gulf,
sensing in your breath the drift
of a lost river that tosses up
as it thunders for sea
its beautiful dream of flight.

SANITARY FISH MARKET AND RESTAURANT, INC. ON THE FABULOUS MOREHEAD CITY, N.C. WATERFRONT

In a flurry of flags we are almost out to sea,
parking the car between masts of unlit lamps,
and when we slam the doors the suns fall off and swim
along the tar. So we walk the white light by smell:
fish, creosote, and then the simpler elements: oxygen,
carbon, sodium. Why don't we just steal a boat?
Why don't we just go out
and let our lungs pump us into origin?
But we go talking, two by two
down a sidewalk that once was sand
straight into the dark that welcomes us
and forgives us as the ocean could not,
a shelter cool and artificial
as we are, to continue our conversation
between mouthfuls of declining species
wrapped in golden wheat, as if we could really harvest
anything we have not made, or really feed
the fraction of our being that is not tears.

DECEMBER TRIPS AND DREAMS

A sister
and I step
into the
hall, deliver
another sister's
baby. We
take it
to my old
room in
the front of
the house
where I was
always afraid
to sleep.

I went to
Denver,
bought a
leather pouch
of marbles
for my son
and for my
daughter,
a beaded
purse. His
was Made
in Haiti,
hers in
Hong Kong.

We leave
two Jewish
children in
the Arab Zone,

run a risk
to save them.
My cousin
talks about
how much
he has changed.

In Atlantic
City we went
to a ca-
sino. We
walked among
the slot
machines and
black jack
tables. A
well-dressed
young man
smiled at
the noise of
cards and
quarters his
excitement
showing through
his trousers.

A thin young
man jumps
about. I
draw back
my fist,
miss and
hit the
lamp as
I wake.

I flew to
Houston,
took a
bus to the
Whitehall
Hotel. My
room had a
bath and
a half and
a black book
of matches
with my
name in gold.

We move in-
to the mansion,
complain at
first about
the eggs our
neighbors
toss. Now
the lawn
is thick
and green.
We watch
cars speed
by behind
the fence.

I remember
it wrong
again. I
change the
words and
tone of
voice, adding
menace and

pain where
none was
meant or
felt. Now
my fears
are justi-
fied.

I remember
flirting with
the waitress
at The Bakery
in Chicago,
the smell
of coffee,
the way she
moved her
hands telling
about dessert,
steam on
windows and
a cold night.

For the first
time in thirty-
nine years, I
like my face—
my beard, my
eyes and
the way they
smile. I like
my boots, too,
and my new
down jacket.
Next month
I will be
forty.

FOR A LAST MIGRATION

Startled geese flush from the blind,
pass without calling
to the stragglers

(no woodsman blurts his warning to the herd—
reluctant caribou steeled for the passage
at the swollen fork
needing their cold now—fearing
breakup, thaw of
the crossing)

Without memory in the brief spring
you whose code lodged in hollow wing bones, in
strength of shoulders, in
the gradual brain faithful lifelong to a mate

you without ambition, adversaries or presidents—

salt flats in which you bred, languorous
marshes of the Virginia shore
vanish as you hatch and fledge
in this stony ground, this northernness—

makeshift travois clatter over black taiga
feral children root in the last stands of birch.

PLANS

This is the way I will do it, she said.
I will go to a place
where I have never been.

I will live in a room
where no one I know
would ever dream of living.

It will be a city I never thought of.
where I know no one,
where nothing will remind me of anything

Or anybody
I have ever known.
I will go there.

She remembers a city
she saw through a train window,
junk in the backyards,

A child's bike
thrown near the tracks.
I'll go there.

She packs her clothes
and moves there
alone.

No one will know
where I have gone.
I will be as empty as the wind.

I will be as unknowing and uncaring
as the Ebro River that flows
through jagged cliffs

Unaware of the still rotting bodies
of Spanish soldiers
in 1938.

I will rid myself
of all memory
and feel nothing

Like the mountains, the glowing stars
and all of nature
that doesn't give a damn

Not even for the people
falling into earth cracks,
in those open mouths

That swallow buildings,
blood and bones
and children

Dissolving them into trembling boiling lava,
the huge earth kitchen
where only cockroaches live.

And she closes her ears and eyes
to everything.
Nothing will remind her…

But the man down the hall
slams the door as her father did
when he would come home drunk.

And then dreams come at night.
She hears the violin next door,
and she sees a boy

Who looks like her brother,
and the voice calling
in the street.

She cannot…
She cannot become the infant
dropped off on the sidewalk.

She hugs the icy lamppost,
her freezing tongue
welded to the black metal.

She hangs on so she will not
fly with the wind.
Memory carries her home again.

MOURNING MUEZZIN: MOGADISHU

Each day
afternoon
gives us sun
hard sand   and
Mogadishu
trees we've cut   return,
ghosts we wish were
green
each day
centuries of barren
afternoon   hot
sun   dry mouth
even our skin
burns in the slash of
wind whipping
sand out of the
eddies and dry
river beds   here
we have built our
houses thick
against the noon
here we have
found ways to make
music from our old
skins empty pots and
left over gut   lean
air   and even the
pliant sounds of our mourning
muezzin
is no less
painful   even his
voice
calling for Allah
is no

balm — I remember
a Palestinian woman, a
wrinkled desert woman
sat in her clay house
without windows
without water
without, saying "Sometimes
I think Allah
has forgotten us" sometimes
here in Mogadishu
when blowing wind
is harsh against the
few remaining
trees
when wheat parched
white against brown
earth, shredding,
when Aideed's men
rattle streets with
50 calibre shells
when even those
who have come to feed us
begin to fire
flares and rockets
into our
night
the burn of phosphorous
is nothing
like the
burning dryness
in our hearts

THE UNEXPLAINED TERRITORIES

I eat poetry for breakfast
in the pink and silver diner
that floats atop a bank of the Susquehanna
lifting crisp words like cereal
into my mouth with sweetrolls and doughnuts.
My waitress wears an angel pin
on the corner of her collar.
If someone gives it to you, she explains,
no harm will come. The angel will
follow, above your shoulder. The cigar smoke
of the grizzled man next to me rises
effortlessly up the mirrored walls
into the fluorescent eaves. He kicks
his caked mudboots against the rail as I say
the poem on the back of a book to myself,
mouthing its words that are otherworldly as mist
on the river studded by dark tree stumps.

"The lady in blue," someone says, and I see
her, sudden, sprouted like an angel
from the right shoulder of the waitress,
or like the precise word I needed
flashing onto a page.   The world reflects
no sorrow today only the gaudy jukebox
spitting out songs, a hat rack covered with mufflers
and berets, my head filled with the music
of possibility as I twirl on a spinning stool,
not knowing what to eat next, another poem,
the feast of trees, the galaxy of mirrors spinning
plain bodies and faces above the counter, and through
the window a river touched with white mist
as miles pass and spill through the window.
I push through the revolving door,
the tired parking lot then enter my car
and move, the teeth of its hood devouring
the unexplained territories.

BLOOD THIRST

We are the broken homing pigeons, carrying all
our backs will bear, wings held wide and open,
mothers rising over the flat roof tops of cities,
caught in the smoking, spinning tails of jets,
our stars, the spark of metal
splitting stars apart.
                              Over Lockerbie, daughters drop
in rain fall, the turning, drying, noon day dust swallows
what breaks, watch face, crystal, the glint, clean light
of grass touched by glass. Who stoops to sort the stone
from bone knows in the brambles what will not go away,
the sudden lurching flash of light, night becoming liquid
day, nothing ever is the same, broken, broken.

To loosen the bands around our legs, dull
the keen scent of what it is that draws us,
blood to blood, over mountains and oceans,
a black weight thickening in the pit of our gullets,
mother beaks leaning into the wind. What unknown hands
will take from us and make of us, our splayed feathers
cannot acknowledge, blood thirst burns beneath our tongues,
hungry for our own, we will circle forever the night sky,
under our breasts, our hearts, the knots of muscle darkening.

FALL MIGRATION AT BRIGANTINE

Instinct is just a word for comings and goings
we can't explain. November brings snow geese
to where the Jersey shore begins or ends,
this unison of marshgrass and mudflats.
And we too have come, a busful
up from the Smithsonian
in boots, plaid hats and binoculars,
our own brand of protective coloration,
eager for a peek at a green-winged teal
among the pintails, or a great blue
fishing from his standstill in the shallows.
Before the bus had left downtown someone
checked off *rock dove* and *ring-billed gull*.
Now a coot stalks the mudbank on galoshy feet
while redtails and turkey vultures
kettle high and slow along the thermals.
Across the bay the casino skyline rises
bluish in the haze. There are thresholds
everywhere but no clear lines:
land and water, fresh and salt, wilderness
and honkytonk. A season, this,
for crossing-over: Tundra swans come
and snow geese by thousands down from the Arctic
turn mudflats to a white shimmer. Look!
Another flock, high enough for twilight,
glittery wingbeats trembling the dark sky,
willed south by wind, shoreline, loss
of light, and ancient pulls we nearly remember—
we who have gathered to watch
and call them by name.

Holy
earth

THE WEEKLY LOAF

Every week I buy a fresh loaf of bread
and score it with lines
marking the seven days
so as not to feast now
and go hungry by Sabbath.
Then I go about my work
with an eager mind. I brush

my black pen through the words
of others, teach myself
patience. I push
through the pages at night,
hunting glimmers
and clues. If the mind
can nourish itself,

the strength of the body
will follow. This I believe—
as an answer must flow
from the shape of its question,
the syllogism of the tree
assume the sun. Each man's life
is a loaf he is given

to hoard or spend
as he will. But the mind
is a chasm, an empty
vessel, a rift in the earth
dark wind blows through. To feed
this glutton, I am frugal,
I busy myself with laws. I scrimp

to make a generosity
of what I am, a fullness
out of hunger. The good Lord
made the earth in seven days.
I carve these lines in the crust
like commandments and follow them well,
so as not to exceed each day's measure.

TOWARD EVENING

Toward evening I begin
to miss the earth   its small shudder
as it turns in its cradle
of liquid air   the odor
of matted fibers decaying   the outlines
of leaves saying   *I am the name*
of your harvest   spores sending up
their everlasting notes   I open
the door of my house and call
the earth back   First the roiling
molten core comes hesitantly   then
the mantle glides
over it like a shoe to its foot   then stones
back into the riverbed   water
and the firmament of water   you know
the story

When I have assembled the earth
I step out into its offerings   I kneel
in the rain touching the tawny
surface the gills of mushrooms the way
you might reach out idly
to touch an animal who knows you   my fingers trace
the patches of universal veils   gemlike
crusts so deadly
and so beautiful   torn ring and sheathing
cup of the destroying
angel   I don't want to be
afraid of what grows here
not of these bright shapes burrowing
into air nor what the body offers

Toward evening when I begin to miss
the earth   when the center of the yew fills
with dark   and a light green presence gathers
at its edges like filaments
or tendrils or cilia sweeping over the air
as if to move an ovum through
great fan-shaped openings on its downward
journey   I end the withholding   wrap
the cloth of darkness around me   in the free
fall into dark the earth's body moving
against gravity rises toward me
and whatever principle governs our two bodies
joined as if they have arisen
from the same spawning   holy earth
who at evening I long for
and go out to

THE GIFT

The Riddle

My coat is paper
You strip it off to get to the
flesh underneath. Each layer
is like the next—you peel
and peel trying to get
to the core, the flame
at the center, but I am all one:
my name means union
and shares a root with loneliness.

The Story

Once there was an old woman.
She was rude to the neighbors, she whipped
her children, she kicked the cat.
She was poor and she hoarded what little
she had. But once she gave an onion
to a woman even poorer than herself.
Who can say why?
She gave it grudgingly,
shoving it into the other's
trembling hands. "Take this,"
she said. "It's all I can spare,"
and she turned away, not wanting to see
the flame of hunger in the other's eyes.

That gift was not a turning point.
The old woman was no nicer than before.
Perhaps that night her stew tasted bland
and she regretted the little she'd given.

Her heart and body shriveled
until she was dry as an empty seed pod.
She rattled around for a while,
and then she died.

Her soul hung suspended over the fires
of hell. "Have you ever done a good deed?"
a voice asked. "Just one and you can
be saved." She was about to say no,
she'd done no good in her life,
when she saw an onion dangling on a wire.
She grabbed the onion and swung
away from the flames lapping her legs.
The wire burned her hands, but she
hung on and inched her way to the edge
of heaven. The angels grabbed her
under the armpits, hoisted her up,
and put her to work peeling onions.
They told her that when she finds
the core of one, she'll see God.

Though her eyes are full of tears,
she is happy with her abundance of onions.
Sometimes she gives them to the cherubs
and they eat them like apples.
When she hears their teeth crunch
the pungent flesh, she smiles
and thinks, "They are eating God."

HANNAH

1st Samuel 1:1-28

The woman I'd recently met was telling me
the story of Hannah, the second and barren wife
of an upright man, Elkanah. The other wife
sneered at Hannah about her lack of children.
And Hannah went to the temple to Eli the priest
and made a vow (he thought she was drunk at first)
that if the lord gave her a son (of course a *son)*
she'd "give him unto the Lord."

                  My new friend continued:
"And she came home and the Bible tells us, 'her husband
knew her' and…and …" her voice trailed off,
"and…'the Lord remembered her.'
Think of it, Bob, the Lord remembered her."
My friend swallowed hard, blinking. "Excuse me," she said,
"I always get this way thinking of Hannah."
Finally she managed to say, "Her son was Samuel."
That was the story. A barren woman saved.
I too felt for Hannah, not so deeply as she.
I, a man, across the chasm, trying.
Perhaps she was thinking of her own past, something in it.
Or of just what women know that men don't know,
women who want children.

VISION

A welter of color inside—diuretics,
tranquilizers, tetracycline—the chassid's

pillbox seems made for a child to play with.
The capsules, like marbles to roll, candies

to suck. He also uses insulin, buys it
in bulk with a gross of needles. All this

to survive the body's storms—rain slashing
like knives, snow swirling in hyperborean blasts.

He'd will an end, were there a passing through
for sure, some delectable houri, waiting even for

a Jew. *Shalom*! she'd say, eternally ready
with the hips. When his virtue slips, he studies

Torah, Talmud. Judah Ben Tema, Abtalyon, Hillel
are friends. So is lithium. He seeds the clouds

with it. His libido rises, and the Baal Shem Tov,
guru fron an age of werewolves, warlocks dances

once again in the Carpathian Mountains, drawing
souls together. *Likut nitzotzot*: the in-gathering

of dispersed sparks. *Come*! He beckons from
across centuries, the pockets of his black vesture

filled with holy miracles. Then, like a presti-
digitator, he's gone. In a test-hospital, aka/gehenna

the man with the pillbox screeches. Figures
in white float by him with words, potions, needles.

His eyes shut defensively, right arm, left
poked, prodded. Elusive are the arteries to God.

EASTER SUNDAY

I miss Him. But He's here,
I've been told. The greatest guitar player
in the world. Wallace Stevens, his hand
at the helm in a world
where a litany is a litany of bad weather,
couldn't compete with His fate. All my
life I've heard this. I don't know

what to believe anymore. I struggle
down sand to the Potomac
and see young boys hooking
silver herring with three-pronged hooks
and immigrant Indians scooting along the shore
on their haunches picking them up
to eat. Where is anybody to tell them
this is wrong? That this is not
the Ganges? That nobody starves in America?
Then one boy turns to me and holds a fish,
pierced through its middle,
high in the sunlight. I miss

Him. The most fat moon does not
resemble Him nor the least
sliver of heartbreak. If I talk enough
about Him He will say something
because I will have been so wrong. I hope
this.

THEY KNEW IT WAS CHRISTMAS

Two girls waked that morning to music.
Blanketed warm, hand in hand they stood
faces against icy panes
looking to the miracle.
Jesus was there bright and real,
His light the street lamp shining
as all about Him flakes fell softly
lest they harm the Baby.
Beneath Him carol singers filled
the blue-white gap with word of birth
and of peace crystal in new snow.

FOR A FRANCISCAN BROTHER

So you want to take your life—
three parallel slashes, *three*,
you said, one for you, your spirit,
and the Holy Father.

I remember months ago
you knelt in the Friary, vowed
to follow a life of chastity, poverty,
and humility. After the profession
a woman, moved by ceremony, honored
you with a replica of St. Francis.
You raised the wooden carving
so high that light from a stained-
glass enlivened the deep-set eyes
that seemed to plead for obedience.

My mind whirls back
to the '70s, you in the hospital
again and again, your disease cold
and relentless, pursuing you
even in remission.

This morning
you knelt by the bed to pray
for nourishment, your white gown
a thin shadow of yourself.
Outside, rain soaked the clothes-
line where a stiff breeze swallowed
a shirt and slacks, spun
them into spirited angels.

Tonight in a vision
I see you in a crowd of lepers,

epileptics, children extending
their arms to a religious: you,
in a Brother's habit, move
to the circle's center
like a proud animal. In full
light you shower their hearts
with prayers. The scene
dissolves into a solitary figure
preaching to birds.

       Leaning over a sink,
I douse my cheeks and brow
with water before entering
the studio where I throw
lights onto a half-finished
statue. I encircle the piece
with my palms, carry it
to the work table, let
my fingers stroke the dark
robe, a thin rope coiled
around a delicate waist.

     As I work, I remember
a basilica on Mount Subasio,
dozens of larks flocking
about the feet of a sculpted man
so proud he lifted his eyes
past the grayed and graying
roofs of Assisi into sky
close enough to touch.

Moving toward the table,
I breathe air into the figure.
Though the broken frame
starts to crumble, I steady
my hands and repair remnants

of a condemned body, then return
the sculpture to its resting place
among a gallery of characters.

         Half-asleep,
I watch the other figures
come alive, hoist the Brother
to their shoulders where he
breaks off a piece of sky,
consumes it and spirals
into the clouds, stars,
into white light
where someone told him
he would find a cure.

PROMISE

When I die,
I'll not come back again.
I'll move into the firmament
with a sway of swallows

flying south too late
to escape icicles
that cut their beaks
and send them tumbling

to earth, a mass of broken wings,
or nurse the pelted birds,
hold them in soft hands
then send them winging

off again to court
the fragrance
of wonder, life
circling back.

WHITE ON WHITE

Just in from the snow, my mind
is the white road out there
filling in as it died behind me
all the way home. Perhaps
as it lost its way in and out
it ran out of one kind of time.

I shake and brush my coat
and lashes and stomp my feet
but something is not going to leave.
The white star lights
I may once have steered by
still fall down streets
and lawns and down behind my eyes,
down optic caves, like galaxies
receding into a rim of space.
White has followed me home from the snow.

I listen here behind the door in the dark:
nothing up the sky is so far out
that its soundings cannot resonate
the stillest mind: and now I know deep
that the white in my yard is not still:
its mass is energy, it lies
like the black holes implicit for years
in Einstein's abstract equation
lying there quiet on paper. I hold on
tight along an icy curve of thought:

That there's some eighth day of the week
inside the window reflection that jumps
into place as I flick on the light: there
for a second my brown coat is raining, my hood
is still tied, the monk I was is humming soft
as candleflame to a white figure rising from white.

dear Mark

even the trees are yours,
your eyes as wise as the woods.
the sound of birds in morning
comes fresh through the light you draw.
how I long to move beneath you in dreams,
see your arms outstretched like two kites,
wings extended to full form, lifting me up
onto the shoulders of my tired song.

at night I search the sky for faces,
but the sun is a clock and we are nowhere,
nowhere as a house on a street where the stove is cold,
and only the poem is brave.
I imagine the soul a small bird,
a soul bird hopping tree to tree,
its strangeness, its beauty—
and on its way it is spilling songs
and it is spilling stones
until we half believe in light.
once, I hit my head against a stone,
thinking this the correct response,
until I found,
it's all in the responding.

LETTER FROM THE CORINTHIANS

Paul:
against

your stiff
wishes

we still
savor

the dictionaries
of desire—

fennel & jasmine
& coriander

for the deeper
our days

slip into winter
the more

my cold palms
read

like a
calendar.

Brothers,
(they say)

we will miss you
for this city

the body, is built
trembling

of red
clay &

wrought tall
with veined ivy.

Therefore,
therefore the birds

of prey
gathered

at our window
may find

fault
with your

apocalypse,
however

shrewdly
executed.

For one thing
(they sing)

your articles
of faith

would not save
even one

drop of blood
dying at the bottom

of my bowl
of cherries.

For another,
all the angels

we fly with
freely

admit
God

is no horror-monger
gorged on hate

but a slim
gourmet

secretly
addicted

to Florentine
strawberries

dipped in
Grand Marnier.

Besieged
by want
and want
and want

SUPEREGO SERENADE

Call me vicious rigid but each and every
moment I'm besieged by want and want and want
you greedy child your plump fist in your mouth
if not for me you'd eat a tree a house gulp
down the very world itself and I know even if
you don't that inside every fat woman is
a fatter one so bless me now and keep your foul
tongue furled inside your mouth I'm here to teach
control to take control and if I sometimes squat
to hold you down I'm no pansy I can take your
rage and dish it out you pig you cow you two bit
whore of Babylon who'd take a crack at every
hunk who's got two balls inside his pants it's up
to me to ladle guilt and blame and don't and don't
to chill you with an image of your mother who's realer
than your mother though she'll be blowzy cheap
and flicking ashes on your cheek you'll know
she's out to kill you with that dagger tucked
inside her stockinged thigh her smartly crayoned
eyebrows cut a jagged pathway to her temple so
reap your just desserts for lusting after taken
men for boys for old old men and as an encore
I'll send in my hit squad to gun you down and for
the mop-up job here comes the crocodile with snapping
jaws you'll wake up with the sweats but fess up
you're relieved to count on me sure as shootin

CACOPHONIES

> *"Drought-stricken plants emit high-pitched noises*
> *as their cell structure breaks down, and scientists*
> *are trying to determine if the sounds are attracting*
> *destructive insects."*
>
> New York Times, Sept. 4, 1988

Unwatered, vegetables turn vociferous:
dill sighs, lettuce whines, peas pop,
cucumbers spit their own seeds with a ping.

Radishes argue in a dull
bump-bump-bump, an occasional
harumph mistaken for a frog.

Potatoes, parched, grow hoarse.
Corn rattles skeletons of stalks.
Asparagus feathers shriek.

Bean tendrils scratch their poles
like fingernails on blackboards.
Chard snarls, tomatoes rage,

turnips growl, zucchinis scream,
watermelons bellow, rutabagas roar,
pumpkins boom, burst in a frenzy of seeds.

Gone mad with thirst
even weeds hardy in heat
put up a racket.

And, circling in formation,
lexicons of insects mass,
mandibles clicking, clicking.

OFFICE

I am still here trying to leave, clearing the debris
and gathering my things for the weekend's work.
This is the end of chaos, I tell myself,
making orderly piles—reports here, memos there,
letters to answer, manuscripts to edit.
My briefcase is open. Feed me, it says calmly,
And I do, taking the first pile and fitting it neatly in.
And then the second and the third. Feed me, it sings,
I love work. The briefcase is full, so I open another,
stuffing it full, but it too is not large enough.
And now I am cramming another—
papers to be edited, articles
I have clipped, bills I have not paid, books that have
sat like stones—they are spilling out on the floor now.
Me too, me too, they cry out, yowling like cats,
I am stuffing and stuffing—there is no end—
and trying to back out of the room,
briefcases hanging from my arms, my back, my legs
like the souls of the dead who cannot let go.
Don't leave us behind, they are shouting.
You want too much, I cry, unable to leave,
their claws tearing my skin. That's not so, they reply,
you can do it, take us. But where, I ask.
Wherever you are going, they cry. But I don't know
where that is, I plead, wanting them only
to understand. Listen to me, please,
I am sorry, but I cannot do it
I cry. But you can, they scream, clinging tighter
and tighter pressing me down under their desperate need.

STILL LIFE WAITING FOR SOMETHING
TO START AGAIN

There's a tight red bowl on the sill
near a rocking chair that's newly painted blue.
Nothing moves, not even a mind,
and if perhaps a spider behind the wall,
so still you'd hear it. The step
on the stair is the wind, only the wind.

When he scoured the sink to white,
hours ago, water rang against rust
in the pipes like a finger rubbing
the rim of a crystal glass.
He won't ask her where she's been,
the years. He made the idea of goblet
spill out on the table the idea of water,
but that was hours ago. There's still a trace.

An emptiness her size and shape
would move now to the window if he were God.
The centerpiece basket holds the woven
shape of the light from the open window
against the dark that starts to struggle
up from the street. She can see the long-gone
tram-track where it crossed itself
on its knees under gaslights, before their time.

The room holds its breath, its little tongues,
the bowl holds air like the open
throat of a bird just before it cries out.
That click and then that click
is the weather checking the steampipes
and it's a long time since he turned a page.
He has dusted everything, hours ago, he has
set the table for two, and now. Now it is time

GREED

The mailman brings midwinter catalogues.
Snow lies deep on the ground. It's bitter cold.
I want everything...

From Wayside Gardens: dictamnus, the gas plant.
"A match held at the base of the flower spike
will ignite the gas the plant exudes." White flowers, dark
green leaves. "Once planted, do not disturb." Will it explode?
Wildflowers: bleeding heart, snakeroot, trillium, phlox,
astilbe, veronica, bunchberry. I want them all...

"Enjoy the freshest, sweetest berries from your garden."
I will. I will. These strawberries surely won't
succumb to drought or mold. Kiwi fruit?
Never mind they won't grow this far north. I'll
plant them anyway. "One male will pollinate
six or seven females for a prodigious harvest." Ah.

From Breck's: the bulbs. Just when I think
my last year's hopes have failed. I'll try again.
Naturalize daffodils across the lawn...
perhaps a lake before them to reflect?
Tulips: Emperors, Queens of Night
Princesses beside Red Matadors. Court Ladies,
Parrots, Artists, Attila and Apricot Delight.

The Metropolitan Museum offers Van Gogh's
gardens, Arles' brilliant painted meadows.
The catalogue has them for jig-saw fans.
Monet observed the light at Giverny
gilding the pale pink lilies in his pool.
They're posters now.

And more. Polymer saints and virgins, knife
handles, animal netsukes, Blue William and his friends,
covered with lotus. And a bowl, a fat
earthenware belly set on bare human feet....

A SUBSIDY ON HONEY

A subsidy on honey
May seem very funny
To people who talk on TV
But consider the tree
In need of a bee
To insure it posterity
The standard Manhattan without a cherry
And no lemon peel for the dry Martini
The empty hive, the Exiled Queen
The disconsolate drone,
The last clover sown
And in search of one flower
When he was last seen
Albert Gore wandering
Through that dismal, gray,
Terminal and silent Spring.

FAWN HALL AMONG THE ANTINOMIANS

"And I can type," she boldly said
With a toss of her carefully tousled locks.
"Smuggle papers and run the Xerox."
"And I know how and what to shred,
For I am an Antinomian."

She never turned brave Ollie's head
For he honored all his oaths, he said,
Unless directed by some authority
That gave lying a higher priority,
Sustained, as he was, by the Fifth and immunity
And basic Antinomian impunity.

Admirable, Admiral John Poindexter
Came with his lawyer, his pipe
And his clerical wife.
Certain he knew what the President thought
He wrought a deniable, plausible plot
Never thinking that he'd be caught
In his Antinomian coup d'etat.

IN THE PICKLE FACTORY

Telling a joke to announce his presence,
even one liked and funny,
the desire evades him on the telephone.
Chatting on as the story tempts,
left reclining in his memory.
The jokes, a habit of gifts he traded,
counting the laughs as a reward
in social pleasure of shared vulgarity.

Now no laugh,
no relief needed.
Seeking no backslap, reflectively.
Listening over the wire
to the older friend's account of an aging mother.
Acceptance and weariness
is the lesson—
when you're 50, you become free.
He's quiet, learning.

On a bend, almost 40,
see both ways without quite turning.
He lets the joke hang in back.
The certainty of a laugh is a quick bond
of mutual shock and pleasure,
silliness and a smile
over a fool in a pickle factory,
between people there is nothing more.

He skips the yarn,
to be close and not,
reach and hide,
a little distance betters the odds.

Smiles,
a shoe shine,
neat gray slacks,
anger in a mask.
The outward signs of promise
announcing, "I'm here! I'm here!"
Unreliable crutches.

It changes his walk.
The steps, still shaky,
are quicker and more sure.
Could some nervous smile be lost to time
without feeling haunted.
Giving in to its certainty
there seems so little to lose,
but money he now spends on neck ties.

The joke inside is clutched,
a Milkbone the mailman tosses to a pesky mutt.
What in this story to embarrass the ladies is attractive?
Crass charm in the ways of the world
and a connection with the curiosity
of those in toilet training.

His spot on the globe
marked by a desire to laugh,
anxious, sometimes inept, happy often.
Mother's brains and father's energy,
a Jew with memories
outside looking in in so many ways.

Into this is born some patience,
the inner voice in ill grammar slows
and acceptance arrives so the heart
now mutters in complete sentences.
This balance, novel,
lets him laugh at the joke returned
into a new pocket.

Days start with the words "shit" or "no" in his mouth.
He doubts he would get up without them.
The habits of a lifetime are that—
the rich or lucky turn them into pride.
Now he showers until he smiles.

The mouth is closed around the little tale of humor.
Newly conscious of guarding himself,
the chat goes stale. A slack renewal
that he finds to his liking.
Only the expectation in each meeting makes it sad—
catch a friend, a love, company
in a net of easy laughs.
Surrender the thought.

The things you see with the volume down—
a neighbor's burden and dread,
and the gift of community.
To be comforted by the training of other's suffering
isn't selfish, just responsible.

The old lady was sick,
the friend's unmarried doctor brother carried the load,
claims he hasn't been concentrating on work
and his wife's kids are still in the house.
Looking neither up nor down,
worries and just too busy.

After a month the story still nags.
It's funny and he wants to tell it
but doesn't make the call.
It won't go stale in his head.
Harping on an old joke is a secret that can't be shared,
so he grins alone.

When the phone rings,
he answers with cheer
and the burp of contentment,
now into a closed fist—
good breeding,
finally prepped for middle age.

NEEDING TO DREAM

When I close my eyes I see
them: the mermaids perched
in the trees in my yard
braiding young branches

and singing not sounds
of words more like bird songs
calling to each other. Then
the waterfalls flow up not

down, disappearing into sky
like racing jetstreams spilling
up into the celestial pool
great sky streams rippling away

and so I fly by saying I can
tight with concentration burning
until I rise up with a great
deep breath (a balloon) holding

all my spirit to fly and follow
the streams and swim the sky
and hear the still underwater
deafness that I have enjoyed

at certain known depths then
I come gasping onto the surface
and my house is being tossed
by a roiling but benevolent sea

riding cerulean waves breaking
whipped foamy caps everywhere
forever I am lost but secure
needing to be lost and home

and lost again I strain to see
my way between wants and needs
and reaching from my window scoop
creamy handfuls to my mouth.

KHATUM SPEAKS

Burumchara, Bangladesh
April, 1991

Cover this land with a dark cloth   flat god
thick with fingers   water rises   beating root
and limb against me.   All night you waved

your arms   roofs soared   the door of my home
swung   over me.   Today my legs are knots
in this tree   my wife is a thread I hold

in my mouth.   Where float the hands
of my children   their shadows I peeled
from my skin to feed your ravenous tongue?

THE OTHER WOMAN

She is stirring today
this one left from another life
restless and still hungry.
Her name given up for a righteous man
his wish filled her every breath
her loss, a slice of every sigh.

    Left to gather it all back in
    I crave the open mouth of alone
    feeding myself sleep or books
    creamed coffee at noon
    time by my own arrangement
    I own few things
    fill rooms with flowers and light.

Surely she sang his children deep into dreams
split fruit open,
sucked on its sweetness
just to be sure for them
spent dim nights mending
her whole body an ache of never enough.

    I know she is with me here
    watching as I pour into spaces
    morning like a warm syrup
    mapled and thick
    moment mixed with moment
    simmering to a richness.

ESTRANGED: kin

Twisted mesh of mangled wreck. Your black silk and gunboat boots.
Two kids and a car. Two lines and nothing said. So I fall back
upon your habitat. This jungle leaves my mind in your vine.
This is our playground. Disneyland. Graceland. Vineland. Drink in.
For the single cost of admission you can fly to the moon, kiss the earth
goodbye.

Face down. Blood pool. I hide my stash, my jeans. You slash your sash.
This is ropeworld. Violent, twisted, and calm. Buy me another drink.
Tip over my yes. Fold my face, softly. Oh, beauty. Justice.

Thank you for taking the time to string me out. Along our heritage
I've come to know home. Grafted, sediment, and kind. I shake
your hands, you kiss my cheek. A small admonishment demonstrates care.

For this a life becomes paper. Nothing more. Home and harm.
Beautiful meals, broken dishes. I adopt a straight line.
Here we are placid. Glass, turbulent, deep. Tide upon the sand. Bound.
Breaking to speak. Learning to scream.

STAY HUNGRY

It means
    eat whatever's eating you,
down to the bone & eat the bone,
savor, grow

    take grass if the rabbit's gone,
multiply & climb, latissimus, tricep,
trapezius, mastoid

    hunger makes it happen, not fondue,
the daily bread your teeth

    diet unless it's you
and you are what you eat,
eat slow, especially the new things, slim

    don't look now, eat everything,
it's eating you, hunger, that's all

    we know you by your bite, let's see:
now count your teeth, how old are you?

    man in a boat, girl in the moon,
hello, goodbye

    longing even after, like dessert,
whatever later eats the pilgrim

It means
    that something got away,
you can almost taste it, why? delectable?
the big rock-candy mountain?
or a street called Brandywine because there's not enough

NIXON'S THE ONE

November 8, a cold rain. Hazard discovered
on the blacktop driveway, trying to get the McGovern-
Shriver stickers off his '65 Ford.
The one on the back bumper is already faded,
the red so bleached it could be declaring
Madly for Adlai. It's gummy, it tears.
The two on his wife's car, a new VW
kept dry in the garage, came off easily.
(In August somebody said the VW's
must be coming off the line in Stuttgart
with McGovern-Shriver stickers.
But Nader was right: in collision
with a fat American machine they're murder.

Our battlefields are accidents, too,
human errors like this late one:
we elect to murder, we murder to elect.)

Who were all those cheering on the gray glass
screen last night, loving their violent darling,
America, whom they had married to money?
He couldn't tarry at that feast—when the wine
ran out, they would change blood to money.

Even in the slanting rain, Hazard is aware
of his oilskin comfort. He is comfortably off,
a two-car man. Somewhere he has gotten out of touch.
This morning he is alone in the defoliated
landscape (oh, his family is indoors there,
snug, adapting to the political weather),
the patrol he scouted with, wiped out.
Standing now on the asphalt no-man's-land,
his hands bloodied with patriotic mucilage,
he cannot shake his unpopular conviction
that his nation has bitterly misspoken itself.

Puzzled
by the
missing
constellations

TODAY

Today is one of those days when I wish I knew
        everything, like the critics.
I need a bit of self-confidence, like the critics.
I wish I knew about Coptic, for example, and Shakti Yoga.
The critics I read know them, and they say so. I wish I
        could say so.
I want to climb up some big publishing mountain and wear
        a little skullcap and say so: I know.

Confidence, that's what I need—to know—
And would have if I came from California or New York.
        Or France.
If I came from France I could say such things as, "Art
        opened its eyes on itself at the time of the
        Renaissance."
If I came from California I could say, "Christianity was
        short-circuited by Constantine."
If I came from New York I could say anything.

I come from Minnesota.
I must get a great big book with all the critics in it
And eat it. One gets so hungry and stupid in Minnesota.

CLAMMING

I go digging for clams once every two or three years
Just to keep my hand in (I usually cut it),
And whenever I do so I tell the same story
Of how at the age of four I was trapped by the tide
As I clammed a sandbar. It's no story at all
But I tell it and tell it; it serves my small lust
To be thought of as someone who's lived.
I've a war too to fall back on, and some years of flying,
As well as a high quota of drunken parties;
A wife and children; but somehow the clamming thing
Gives me an image of me that soothes my psyche
Like none of the louder events: me helpless,
Alone with my sandpail,
As fate in the form of soupy Long Island Sound
Comes stalking me.

I've a son now at that age.
He's spoiled, he's been sickly.
He's handsome and bright, affectionate and demanding.
I think of the tides when I look at him.
I'd have him alone and sea-girt, poor little boy.

The self, what a brute it is. It wants, wants.
It will not let go of its even most fictional grandeur
But must grope, grope down in the muck of its past
For some little squirting life and bring it up tenderly
To the lo and behold of death, that it may weep
And pass on the weeping, keep the thing going.

Son, when you clam,
Watch out for the tides and take care of yourself,
Yet no great care,
Lest you care too much and brag of the caring
And bore your best friends and inhibit your children and sicken
At last into opera on somebody's sandbar. Son, when you clam,
Clam.

WAITING

We are always waiting
for that moment to arrive
as it must, irresistibly.
All our lives
we long for the surprise
we've been expecting
for the windfall suddenly
to flash from the skies.
Sitting in a crowded train
or standing alone at a party
in skylit rooms filled
with the patois of false promise,
wherever we are
we never stop waiting
desperately at times
dying for
that voice amid voices
that chance glance
that telephone ringing
in our dark room
on a wet Friday night.
Settling to sleep
we lie there
scanning our best dreams
our most adorable memories
lifted to myth
on the dark wall
playing them
over and over
all night long.
Still, we know, uncurling

from dead
in the unknowable distance,
moments away,
a soft petal will touch us
familiar beyond our dreams.

Or, maybe, when we walk
in the gray woods,
ever alert to the possible,
we will come across a cache
hidden there long ago
by those who couldn't reach it again
no matter how hard they tried
holding it as a treasured loss,
a loss that enriched their lives
with secret knowledge,
as trees in winter
live for the perfect day
when the sun ripens over them
with fragrant light—
and everything is changed
after that
startling into a new life.

And knowing this, we dress
in our daily disguise of blue
or gray, our coat flapping
in the rainy morning
on the platform, waiting
standing with ourselves
our folded newspaper
briefcase at our feet

like a humble dog
we must walk around with
days beyond days without passion,
carrying those stubs that tell us
how much time we have
to use or lose.
And when the train
grumbles toward us
from far away, lights
numbering the ties of the tracks
and arrives at our station
we must know
any moment
the doors will open
and we will go on
as we have.

L. K. DECRIES THE ABSENCE OF PASSION

I have grown unused
to displays of emotion—
outrage, joy and lust,
even greed succumb
to the compromise of his
common sense. How I miss
appetite. Stuck in this
village of incident, how
I long for one tragic weekend
in the city of grand occasion.

Dramatic young men appear
in my peripheral visions.
They find me peevish
and withdrawn, liken me
to a dowager aunt
hiding knives and forks
in pacific cloth
and eating only with spoons.

I would trade this peace
for bouts of screaming
for no reason. I would
confirm again the radical
differences in the temperature
of tears. From where
it rusts in a box, I lift
the old anger out
and sharpen it on the stone
of my deceiving.

DIALECTIC OF THE CENSUS TAKERS

Last night in the dislabor
of falling asleep, I dreamed
my sheep had gone astray
reproducing Fibonacci sums of lambs
which escaped my repose into your wakefulness.

You asked, "The recipe, could I
have the recipe?" Even as my body
made its nightly mends,
I countered, "Formula,
you do want the *formula*?"

You sulked,
"I thought you were hungry too."
From the wool of every bleating ewe,
a mathematician sprang
Archimedes, Newton, Gauss.

"More," they demanded. "More."
The sheep couldn't keep pace
with their ability to count.
But you insisted,
"I didn't have enough."

In this world, not all of us
can find our own nourishment.
Hunger keeps us awake.
But tonight, dear Friend,
the sheep are somnambulating

from my pillow to yours.
There is nothing to do
and nothing to eat—
nothing, nothing
but sleep.

HARD DIRT

Just suppose I am weary,
working to catch every drop
of water. I am guardian
of a small continent,
a slab of hard dirt
pressed in on itself,
almost impervious to water, to life.

Sisyphus nods as I haul
a wooden bucket filled with water
from a distant land. The road
is unmarked; the bucket leaks.

Just suppose this had not been true. How
would I have learned to live?

ENUNCIATION

He is my student of the five senses:
a seventeen-year-old boy, two years into America,
out of Sierra Leone. His language is not here,
and his tongue meets words they have to know
but do not meet the sense of: olfactory, larynx, neuron.

Avoiding my eyes, he words the book,
asking it to speak, spare him as middle man.
My inward net casts far into a clear pool,
pulls up stars of words, a gurgle of laughter.

He knows what walking means to legs. He knows without a
heart,
we would be like the tiny ants. Without a brain
we would be like our books, telling without saying
a page of eyes with no sight.

He could draw me his meanings,
he could tap them with his feet like any young boy.
We depend on waves, the wanting, the letting go,
a nod that means no while it says yes,
a blank.

We are waiting at the foot
for the mountains to send wind.

THE IMPORTANT THINGS

she wanted to name a child Cosmo or Delilah or Ustis
something grand and memorable
she wanted a son taller than she a football-playing son
a blonde son
she wanted to be a star in the evening sky
the one that everyone sees
she wanted to get married just for the memory
to have a bouquet of long white roses to throw
and a thousand-dollar gown
she wanted to lust after someone dark and greasy
someone wrong for her definitely wrong
she wanted to kiss a stranger a man
or a woman kiss them hard
then walk away into a crowded street a parade
and become someone's dream
she wanted long curly red hair and big boobs
and perfect nails
she wanted women to envy her no to hate her
she wanted to drive a blue Porsche
down to the very edge of the Grand Canyon alone
she wanted to be Jacques Cousteau and
she wanted to roam the Alps
she wanted to live in a cave in India for forty years and
talk until the sun rose with the Dalai Lama or
someone dead magical and dead
she wanted a guru and she wanted God
she wanted God to visit her in her cave
to give her messages special secret messages
she wanted to die to be buried at sea
to have fish peck at her until she was bone
bone white and covered with weeds
most of all she wanted to remember
the very moment she was born

IN THE NOCTURNAL ANIMAL HOUSE

A trick of light brings them
here into this open space
where they're vulnerable.
In the dim infrared they

hunt, evade, forage
as if unseen,
mate, grieve,
(These the hours of being born,
these the hours the traps are filled.)

They are puzzled by the missing
constellations, the way their enemies
hover yet stay off,
never arriving,

the presence of unscarred old ones
and young not protected by fear;

the constant weather,
changes in their
bodies bearing no correspondence
to the light:

(Leaves perfect, unmoved by wind.)
the coat thickening,
the warning senses
dulling, the inescapable

sleepiness, the need
to leave this benign landscape
together, traveling quickly
in a single direction.

LATE AT NIGHT

Wind at the window   a chain saw
cutting glass. Imagine me a soothsayer
practicing without a license, addicted
to darkness. Those familiar sounds
erode loneliness, water flushing,
footsteps on the stair, slippered feet
on Sarouk, sleep noises, swallows of air,
flashes of light. The tall case clock
that was my father's lights up phases
of the moon, chimes the quarter hour.

I listen for the snowy-headed hoot owl,
silent as a well fed cat. Colors turn
red as the crested cardinal flitting
from bush to tree. Though I have
never seen hens in the barnyard
protect their young from marauding
foxes or heard a cock crow, I can stay
this course until morning. In Kenya
where I have never been, zebras
and giraffes move noiselessly
in pairs across the Serengeti.
Rousseau's lion sleeps in the tall grass.

At dawn, the wind chill charged with light,
I, dazzled by sun, face the equator, measure
the international date line. Kilimanjaro,
too high to climb, my hunger too great
to appease. What's that line from *White Mischief*?
Another fucking gorgeous day in Paradise.

ON A BEACH IN SOUTHERN CONNECTICUT

Gradually the monotony of his rhythms
overwhelmed him, like the repetition of small waves
on a beach in southern Connecticut.
This had been good, a good; but moderation
in excess, even the moderate luxury
of a rocky coast, became, finally,
one lesson in the same, old discipline:
excess leading to wisdom, and what good is wisdom?

The circles superimposed themselves, the sun
superimposed itself, on the same spot,
in the same sky, the same, in all practicality,
over the same beach. It was monotonous here
and good; the tempo of the sun was a familiar
tempo, but not a song to dance to.

Any change was needed. Almost any change.
Pacification of the prairie land-wars,
forgetting the skirmishes of cattlemen
and sheepmen, and the insomniac coyote,
had been effected on a furlough by the sea,
a truce. War and a truce were the first lessons:
not variations on a theme, but
alternation of all the possible routines.

If only the sun would bloom again with blood
he might intone a song with consonance.
Or if it shrivelled into haggling
inconsequence—as on a muggy day
a gullish cacophony composes
a rhapsody, for nerves teased into sympathy.

If only he could bring himself to sacrifice
this peace to all that chintz. Of course, to be
truly satisfied would be to forget
one's disaffections, would be to forget
the cult of satisfactions is a cult
and to forget one had forgotten. To forget
to anticipate. To be caught up
in an expanding and contracting

—hunger. He had forgotten lunch
and now it must be nearly half-past four.
Gin and bitters: crackers, triscuit, sea biscuit:
gouda, port salut, cheddar: braunschweiger:
anchovies or smoked mussels: and then dinner.
The old critique of heaven: no hunger. No stomach ache.
        No wisdom. Nothing.

DAYLIGHT SAVINGS

It is time again
to set the clocks forward
in the name of light,
pocket an hour on the sly
and hope no one will notice.

At 2 a.m. the daylight
savers come, who never blink
an eye or dream. They are all business,
paid by the hour,
purse-lipped in silence
while we turn and sleep.

What to do
with the flapping thing now,
this annual appendix.
In the morning it is 9, not 8,
noon, not 11. You rise
and who really is
the wiser, except for the crumbs
and a feather on the floor,
which you try to ignore.

So what if something full and dark
hangs over you all day
and the next, and the next,
trying to tell you
something. So what
if you can't shake it off
and later, don't want to.

So what if the lone hour
they once said
would always be yours
circles above you, loving
and relentless.

THE TAMING POWER OF THE GREAT

One by one, the city's lights assume their places
in the citadel, populating the indigo dusk
like individual intelligences.

Small figures stream out of the mouths of buildings,
a trace of surprise on the glass faces.

In the upper rooms, a hollow rattling of brass,
pressing out against the mirrored windows

(which were not meant to open). Deep in the ziggurat
blind treasures amass—strange currency
awaiting conversion, old tablets awaiting translation.

Treading daily into the wild boar's lair
requires a kind of radical deflection—obsolete now,
the whip and the chair. The lights come up.

The dinner hour descends. The question of nourishment
remains suspended. A tentative wet snow (the season's first)
falls gently, equally, on all the hungers.

THE WASHINGTON WRITERS' PUBLISHING HOUSE
GRACE CAVALIERI • JEAN NORDHAUS

The Early Years
by Grace Cavalieri

1. A Pyramid of Poets

Everything starts with a thought—a simple thought—chairs, babies, poems, and institutions. Thoughts are powerful and they materialize in the world. Sometimes they stay around awhile.

The man with the first thought about Washington Writers' Publishing House was **John McNally**—then a poet, now a lawyer practicing in Vermont. In 1975 I remember sitting at a desk on Connecticut Avenue, in the office of graphic designer **Jim True**, with John. We were talking about how great it would be if Washington had its own poetry press where poets were printed and then joined in the great collaborative (remember this was the seventies!) to work together to run the operations. John was at that time a naval officer on his way to being a law school student at the University of Virginia. He was a great starter of things. We were close friends and were obsessed with this potent thought about writers publishing other writers. A strong motivation was offered by Jim True, the third part of our triumvirate, who had an image of beautiful books he wanted to design. He couldn't wait to get his hands on the paper.

And so it was. The pilot project was to be a model to see where we were going—by going there. I was one of the poets chosen to start the publishing experiment. **Deirdra Baldwin** was another, and the third was **Terence Winch**, who was known for his work with the "Mass Transit" group of poets.

The by-laws were puzzled out, and John, who had one foot in the Law, was very good at it. He became our first president. The by-laws are very detailed and quite masterful, and have since been used as a model for other like ventures. The ruling principle was that each group of poets published would take over the administration of the House until, exponentially, we built an empire—or at least a pyramid of poets—broadbased and far reaching...each writer shouldering the next one. Another basic tenet was that each poet pay one-half the cost of publication and the House furnish the other 50 percent. This was to be a co-op all the way.

And the first editions were beautiful. Three silky books that still feel good in the hand—Jim True's delicately precise cover designs all compatible—my own *Why I Cannot Take A Lover* (blues/stars); Deirdra's *Gathering Time* (green/spheres); and Terence's *Luncheonette Jealousy* (mauve/hearts). The print font—in keeping with the overall look of the chapbooks—is still pristine and elegant.

We employed a unique method of book distribution in those days. Deirdra would double-park her car outside of a bookstore (later we'd get our friend **Robert Sargent** to be the getaway man) and I'd run in and sneak a handful of books onto the shelf—and then I'd escape. We called it the "Drop-and-Split Method" of book distribution, and, as far as we know, the bookstores sold all the books. We got no money but poetry was on the streets.

In 1977 I became president of WWPH in keeping with the pyramid theory of management, and Deirdra's friend **Roberta Pilk** became secretary. Our small cadre opened solicitation. Although John McNally was a shoo-in (*Northern Lights*), three other male authors were chosen from submitted manuscripts, and, although Robert Sargent already had my vote (for *Now Is Always the Miraculous Time*), I remember Deirdra giving a long enraptured speech on formalism in his behalf. I was pushing **Ron Rodriguez**, whose book title, *The Captains That Dogs Aren't*, tells a little about his sensibility. The additional selection was **Harrison Fisher**'s book, *The Gravity*. Bobby Pilk's mother was an artist and these editions became slim, beautiful, beige volumes, with line drawings of our poets on their covers.

In 1978 Robert Sargent became president and he took piles of notes and papers—applying his engineer's brain to the House by actually alphabetizing files and keeping a ledger. There was nothing to do but make him treasurer too. I stayed on as vice president through the wonder years, enjoying the astral plane of poetry, while Robert became long its servant, bringing to our art his exactitude—and working good-naturedly as bookkeeper, chauffeur, and senior editor.

While it is true that we started as a raggedy band of poets kicking up our own stardust, we soon settled down to the business of establishing some principles of poetry selection and publication that still exist today. Although we publicized competition deadlines, we did not request manuscripts from individuals. This was a mixed blessing, because although it established a totally objective course of travel, it also limited judging only to what was submitted. We had to hope that we would evolve toward the intergenerational, multi-dimensional institution we knew we could become—and finally are happily becoming.

The review process took shape so that each member read each manuscript separately, rotating until we all read everything. Each of us wrote long notes on the poetic elements we saw within the manuscripts. There were final readings with the poetry that had floated like cream to the top. Then the editorial board had many discussions at the table about the qualities of each potential book. Disappointed applicants could reenter the following year, and many, to our satisfaction, did. It was a process of the highest probity.

That year (1978) we published **Patrick Clary** (*Notes for a Loveletter*), **E. Ethelbert Miller** (*Migrant Worker*), and **Katherine Cobey** (*Thrift*). Somewhere along the line Deirdra started up The Word Works Press, but we never saw it as competition. She just went from one press to the other as time and energy allowed. I was trying to get a new radio station ensconced on the air while moving to work full-time at PBS. We had incredible fun in those years, with meetings of high idealism, intensity, and sometimes hilarity, mostly in Robert Sargent's apartment.

In 1979 Robert and **Octave Stevenson** (then Director of Literature, Martin Luther King Memorial Library) took on a monumental editing project—an anthology of Washington writers. The book was entitled *The Poet Upstairs*, after a line taken from a John Pauker poem. The anthology celebrates 110 poets in nearly 200 pages. It is still a benchmark in Washington small press activity. For the next five years, Robert stayed at the helm as president and treasurer; I hung in as vice president. Bobby Pilk stayed as secretary until 1982, when she turned her tasks over to **Mary Riser**.

2. Like Cream to the Top

The years immediately following turned out additional significant poets: 1979—**Beth Joselow**, **Catherine O'Neill**, and **Shirley Cochrane**; 1980—**David Bristol**, **Greg Hannan**, and **Gray Jacobik**; 1981—**May Miller**, **Judith Harris**, and **Beate Goldman**; 1982—**Hastings Wyman, Jr.**, **Mary Ann Larkin**, and **Elisavietta Ritchie**.

Robert Sargent gave up the presidency in 1983 (although he stayed on as treasurer, and we made him do all the work anyway), and the presidents were then, for the next several years, Shirley Cochrane, Hastings Wyman, Jr., Lisa Ritchie, and Eric Nelson.

In 1983 the press published its eighth series, with volumes by **Paul Estaver**, **Eric Nelson**, and **Catherine Harnett (Shaw)**. In 1984, Series IX brought forth books by **Elaine Magarrell** and **David McAleavey**. We can't remember why there were no WWPH publications in 1985—finances, no doubt—but Series X resumed in 1986 with poets **Ann Darr** and **Barbara Lefcowitz**, followed in 1987 by **Myra Sklarew** and **Jean Nordhaus**; 1988, **Maxine Clair** and **Ann Knox**; 1989, **Martin Galvin** and **Sharon Negri**.

Jean Nordhaus became president in 1989, bringing new vigor to the organization. Robert Sargent stayed in office as treasurer for one final year. This brought us into a new era, the nineties, with a fully developed publishing operation. The Washington Writers' Publishing House is now an *institution*, a permanent one, a respectable public venture publishing some of the most interesting writers from the Greater Washington metropolitan area. Distribution is no longer a drop-and-split escapade. WWPH poets are routinely invited to bookstores to read, to converse, and to sign their own books.

It is institutional small press publishing all the way. We have a new look of unity for our books thanks to the graphic design expertise of **Jeanne Krohn**. And what a contribution WWPH makes to our city—to know that everyone in its environs has a fair chance to compete for publication of handsome editions that are properly marketed and reviewed. Now we have committees and deadlines, a sign, I guess, of growing older—maybe wiser. We have expanded our efforts to include sending our poets into area schools. All this stands only because the cooperative philosophy has remained steadfast throughout the years. And it is that very philosophy that brings us to salute our twentieth year of press publication with this new anthology.

But now and then, I think back 20 years and see myself sitting on the floor of Robert's apartment with Deirdra (now in L.A.) and Bobby Pilk (now gone to Vermont), who were always talking and dancing. This was before we knew it was a time we were to remember. It's only sometimes now, in looking back, that I wish thoughts could stay still a little while—just a little while—longer, before moving off into the remote atmosphere.

Building(s)
by Jean Nordhaus

Is Washington Writers' Publishing House, after 20 years, now an "institution"?

Institutions have heavy mahogany doors, brass railings, and polished floors. Many boast columns. They are banks, libraries, universities, counting houses, and their weightiness bespeaks the conjunction of marble and money. We are a House without a home. What we are—and have been since our beginnings—is a post office box and a network of ongoing personal relationships created by circumstance and sustained by our collective wish that the press continue. Each new book is the opening of a new door.

The nineties have already brought forth WWPH books by
Patricia Garfinkel and Elisabeth Murawski; Laura Brylawski-
Miller and Nan Fry; Joseph Thackery and Naomi Thiers; Barri
Armitage and Elaine Upton; Paul Haenel and Kim Roberts; and
Dan Johnson and Jane Schapiro. The press's first venture into
audio tape publication was Kwelismith's *Browngirl in the ring*.
Although our House is invisible, we are keeping the doors open.

Since 1994, Patricia Garfinkel and Laura Brylawski-Miller
have shared, as co-presidents, the ever-widening responsibility of
running the press. WWPH authors new and old participate in
press functions. There is much to do and much to publish. There's
never enough time! We're hungry for time, hungry for first-rate
manuscripts, hungry for more doors. How hungry? Hungry as we
are. It seems only fitting that WWPH's 20-year publishing anni-
versary take the form of this anthology, filled to bursting with the
work of poets from the metropolitan area, including, of course,
our own press authors.

Back in 1979, among my proudest publications were my early
poems accepted for the press's first anthology. To be included
meant the world to me. WWPH represented hope, an opening
through which I might hope to enter the world of writers. Later,
eight years later to be exact, my book was finally accepted by
WWPH after several earlier attempts. Although I went on to serve
as WWPH president for six years, I have always viewed the press
from the bottom up, from the standpoint of a writer just starting
to reach out and hungry for encouragement.

This new anthology includes poets of local and national
reputation. It embraces beginning poets, several poets laureate,
and Pulitzer Prize winners. The poems were solicited, as is always
our practice, through open entry call, and chosen by committees
of press authors. The anthology may represent hope for some; for
others, an additional achievement. For WWPH, the anthology is a
celebration of our city, its environs, and our collective ability to
grow and flourish as a press.

What will WWPH be in 20 years? *Where* will it be? Surely,
new structures will evolve on the stones of that sturdy pyramid,
constructed two decades ago, of a graphic designer's dream of
beautiful books and poets' dreams of beautiful songs. With luck
and hard work, it will stand through 20 more years.

Karren L. Alenier. "Dialectic of the Census Takers" copyright © 1989 by Karren L. Alenier and reprinted from *Negative Capability* by permission of the author.

Cicely Angleton. "Chrysoberyl" copyright © 1995 by Cicely Angleton.

Barri Armitage. "After Words," "Bedding Down," and "Fitting" copyright © 1993 by Barri Armitage and reprinted from *Double Helix* (WWPH) by permission of the author.

Mel Belin. "Vision" copyright © 1990 by Mel Belin and reprinted from *Phoebe* by permission of the author.

David Bristol. "In the Pickle Factory" copyright © 1995 by David Bristol.

Laura Brylawski-Miller. "The King of a rainy country" and "The stars of the Bear" copyright © 1995 by Laura Brylawski-Miller.

Nancy Naomi Carlson. "Blackberry Jubilee" and "Please" copyright © 1995 by Nancy Naomi Carlson.

Kenneth Carroll. "hungry eyes" copyright © 1995 by Kenneth Carroll.

Grace Cavalieri. "Helpmates" copyright © 1995 by Grace Cavalieri and reprinted from *Lips* by permission of the author. "Tarot Card IV. Emperor" copyright © 1995 by Grace Cavalieri.

Maxine Clair. "First Flame" copyright © 1992 by Maxine Clair and reprinted from *G.W. Review* by permission of the author.

William Claire. "The Jello Man on the Feast of Circumcision" copyright © by William Claire and reprinted from *Chelsea 38* (Chelsea Associates, Inc.) by permission of the author.

Shirley G. Cochrane. "The Candy Queen" and "Water" copyright © 1995 by Shirley G. Cochrane.

Don Colburn. "Fall Migration at Brigantine" copyright © 1992 by Don Colburn and reprinted from *The Iowa Review* by permission of the author.

Gail Collins-Ranadive. "Because of the Starving" copyright © 1988 by Gail Collins-Ranadive and reprinted from *Friendly Woman's Women and Justice Issue* by permission of the author.

Maxine Combs. "Listening for Wings" copyright © 1990 by Maxine Combs, first published in *The Poet's Domain*, and reprinted in *Ruby* and *The Takoma Voice*. "Form and Content" copyright © 1984 by Maxine Combs, first published in *The Round Table*, and reprinted in *Swimming Out of the Collective Unconscious* (The Wineberry Press) and in *Pudding*. Both reprinted by permission of the author.

Christopher Conlon. "Hunger" copyright © 1995 by Christopher Conlon.

Geraldine Connolly. "Dickinson in Winter" copyright © 1995 by Geraldine Connolly and reprinted from *Chelsea*. "The Unexplained Territories" copyright © 1993 by Geraldine Connolly and reprinted from *West Branch*. Both reprinted by permission of the author. "My Mother's Refrigerator" copyright © 1995 by Geraldine Connolly.

Sarah Cotterill. "For a Last Migration" copyright © 1991 by Sarah Cotterill and reprinted from *In the Nocturnal Animal House* (Purdue University Press). "In the Nocturnal Animal House" copyright © 1991 by Sarah Cotterill, first appeared in *Quarry West* and reprinted from *In the Nocturnal Animal House*. Both reprinted by permission of the author.

Katherine Cottle. "Birdman, Springfield Hospital" and "Will Work for Food" copyright © 1995 by Katherine Cottle.

R.F. Coyne. "Boning Knife" copyright © 1995 by R.F. Coyne.

Mary Ann Daly. "Niagara" and "Sanitary Fish Market and Restaurant, Inc. on the Fabulous Morehead City, N.C. Waterfront" copyright © 1995 by Mary Ann Daly.

Ann Darr. "Food" copyright © 1990 by Ann Darr and reprinted from *The Twelve Pound Cigarette* (SCOP Publications, Inc.). "I Have Been Hungry" copyright © 1995 by Ann Darr. "Love Poem" copyright © 1993 by Ann Darr and reprinted from *Confessions of a Skewed Romantic* (The Bunny and the Crocodile Press). All reprinted by permission of the author.

Donna Denizé. "Alzheimer's #1" copyright © 1995 by Donna Denizé.

William Derge. "Tour of Duty" copyright © 1995 by William Derge.

Toi Derricotte. "For My First Grade Teacher and Her Special Messenger" copyright © 1994 by Toi Derricotte and reprinted from *Prairie Schooner*. "Passing" copyright © 1994 copyright © 1994 by Toi Derricotte and reprinted from *The Kenyon Review*. Both reprinted by permission of the author.

Neal Michael Dwyer. "24, Avenue de la Bornala" copyright © 1995 by Neal Michael Dwyer.

Paul Estaver. "Deep Inside Danny But Still Visible Behind the Glasses," "How High the Moon," and "Muldoon, Widower" copyright © 1983 by Paul Estaver and reprinted from *Salisbury Beach—1954* (WWPH). All reprinted by permission of the author.

Roland Flint. "Easy" copyright © 1991 and reprinted from *The Plum Review*. "Love Story" copyright © 1995 by Roland Flint. "Stay Hungry" copyright © 1977 and reprinted from *Dryad*. All reprinted by permission of the author.

Elizabeth Follin-Jones. "At Odds" copyright © 1991 by Elizabeth Follin-Jones, published in *The Maryland Poetry Review*. "Impasse" copyright © 1990 by Elizabeth Follin-Jones. Both reprinted from *One Flight From The Bottom* (Artscape Literary Arts Award) by permission of the author.

Lillian Frankel. "Plans" copyright © 1990 by Lillian Frankel and reprinted from *Lip Service* by permission of the author.

Nan Fry. "The Gift," "The perfect room," and "The Plum" copyright © 1991 by Nan Fry and reprinted from *Relearning the Dark* (WWPH) by permission of the author.

Martin Galvin. "Appetites" copyright © 1989 by Martin Galvin and reprinted from *Wild Card* (WWPH). "Blueberry Woman" copyright © 1989 and reprinted from *Making Beds* (Sedwick House). "Eating London" copyright © 1995 by Martin Galvin. All reprinted by permission of the author.

Patricia G. Garfinkel. "Brain Chemistry," "Genessee Street," and "Hard Dirt" copyright © 1995 by Patricia G. Garfinkel.

Howard Gofreed. "Apostrophe" and "Cicadas" copyright © 1995 by Howard Gofreed.

Sid Gold. "Nice" and "Valentine" copyright © 1995 by Sid Gold.

Barbara Goldberg. "A Matter of Choice" copyright © 1992 by Barbara Goldberg and reprinted from *New England Review*. "Superego Serenade" copyright © 1990 by Barbara Goldberg and reprinted from *The Colorado Review*. "What Is Served" copyright © 1989 by The Modern Poetry Association, first appeared in *Poetry* and is reprinted by permission of the Editor of *Poetry*. All reprinted by permission of the author.

James Griffin. "Waiting" copyright © 1993 by James Griffin and reprinted from *The Maryland Poetry Review* by permission of the author.

Paul R. Haenel. "Easter Sunday" copyright © 1991 by Paul R. Haenel, first published in *hitchhiker* and reprinted in *The Wallace Stevens Journal*. "The Moon on her Birthday" copyright © 1994 by Paul R. Haenel and reprinted from *Farewell, Goodbye, Wave Goodbye* (WWPH). Both reprinted by permission of the author.

Hamod (a.k.a. Sam Hamod). "Mourning Muezzin: Mogadishu" copyright © 1995 by Hamod and reprinted from *Poets Momma Didn't Raise* (Cedar Creek Press) by permission of the author.

Judith Harris. "Maria" copyright © 1995 by Judith Harris.

Clarinda Harriss. "Patch" copyright © 1995 by Clarinda Harriss.

Richard Harteis. "Domestic" and "Insomnia" copyright © 1981 by Richard Harteis and reprinted from *Morocco Journal* (Carnegie-Mellon University Press). "Gibbous" copyright © 1994 and reprinted from *Keeping Heart: New and Selected Roems* (Orpheus House). All reprinted by permission of the author.

reuben jackson. "after frank o'hara" and "anger" copyright © 1995 by reuben jackson.

Josephine Jacobsen. "The Chinese Insomniacs" and "The Suicides" copyright © 1987 by Josephine Jacobsen, first published in *The Sisters* (The Bench Press) and reprinted from *The Chinese Insomniacs* (University of Pennsylvania Press). Both reprinted by permission of the author.

Philip K. Jason. "Wisdom Poem" copyright © 1995 by Philip K. Jason.

Rod Jellema. "Missing Sleep" and "White on White" copyright © 1984 by Rod Jellema and reprinted from *The Eighth Day: New and Selected Poems* (Dryad Press). "Still Life Waiting for Something to Start Again" copyright © 1993 and reprinted from *The Plum Review*. All reprinted by permission of the author.

Dan Johnson. "Attempting Magic" copyright © 1992 by Dan Johnson and reprinted from *Lullwater Review*. "Cave Painter" copyright © 1986 by Dan Johnson and reprinted from *Alioth*. "A House is a Story" copyright © 1992 and reprinted from *Lip Service*. All poems also appear in *Come Looking* (WWPH) and are reprinted by permission of the author.

Joy Jones. "last nite" copyright © 1995 by Joy Jones.

Beth Joselow. "Three Songs" copyright © 1995 by Beth Joselow.

Thomas M. Kirlin. "Banquet" and "Letter from the Corinthians" copyright © Thomas M. Kirlin.

Peter Klappert. "The Flower Cart and the Butcher" copyright © 1984 by Peter Klappert and reprinted from *The Idiot Princess of the Last Dynasty* (Alfred A. Knopf). "On a Beach in Southern Connecticut" copyright © 1971 by Peter Klappert and reprinted from *Lugging Vegetables to Nantucket* (Yale University Press). Both reprinted by permission of the author.

Ann B. Knox. "Aunt from the Country" copyright © 1990 by Ann B. Knox and reprinted from *Carousel*. "She Remembers the First Time" copyright © 1990 by Ann B. Knox and reprinted from *Passager*. Both reprinted by permission of the author.

Carolyn Kreiter-Foronda. "For a Franciscan Brother" copyright © 1988 under the name of Carolyn Kreiter-Kurylo and reprinted from *Contrary Visions* (Scripta Humanistica) by permission of the author.

Kwelismith. "neckbones n sauerkraut" and "soblack" copyright © 1989 by Kwelismith and reprinted from *Slavesong: the art of singing* (Anacostia Repertory Company) by permission of the author.

David Lanier. "What a Penny Bought" copyright © 1995 by David Lanier.

Mary Ann Larkin. "George Yater's Self Portrait—1930" copyright © 1995 by Mary Ann Larkin.

Barbara F. Lefcowitz. "The Blood Tree" copyright © 1995 by Barbara F. Lefcowitz.

Merrill Leffler. "Gift" and "Office" copyright © 1995 by Merrill Leffler.

Ellen Mauck Lessy. "Courses" copyright © 1994 by Ellen Mauck Lessy and reprinted from *MEDIPHORS: A Literary Journal of the Health Professions* by permission of the author.

Lyn Lifshin. "My Mother Wants Lamb Chops, Steaks, Lobster, Roast Beef" copyright © 1991 by Lyn Lifshin and reprinted from *Ploughshares*. "Potato Peels" copyright © 1995 by Lyn Lifshin and reprinted from *Blue Tattoo* (Event Horizon Press). Both reprinted by permission of the author.

Carmen Lupton. "Carcass" copyright © 1995 by Carmen Lupton.

Mariquita MacManus. "This Uncommon Banana" copyright © 1995 by Mariquita MacManus.

Elaine Magarrell. "Chrysanthemums," "The Gym," and "L.K. Decries the Absence of Passion," copyright © 1995 by Elaine Magarrell.

Veneta Masson. "Deliverance" copyright © 1995 by Veneta Masson. "The Promise" copyright © 1994 by JAMA and reprinted from *Journal of the American Medical Association*. Both reprinted by permission of the author.

David McAleavey. "Lunchbox" copyright © 1985 by David McAleavey and reprinted from *Holding Obsidian* (WWPH) by permission of the author.

Richard McCann. "Lace" and "One of the Reasons" are reprinted from *Ghost Letters* (Alice James Books). Copyright © 1994 by Richard McCann. "Lace" originally appeared in *Shenandoah*. "One of the Reasons" originally appeared in *The Virginia Quarterly Review*. Both reprinted by permission of the author.

Eugene J. McCarthy. "Fawn Hall Among the Antinomians" copyright © 1980 by Eugene J. McCarthy and reprinted from *The New Republic*. "A Subsidy on Honey" copyright © 1979 by Eugene J. McCarthy and reprinted from *Ground Fog and Night* (Harcourt Brace). Both reprinted by permission of the author.

Judith McCombs. "Epithet" copyright © 1990 by Judith McCombs and reprinted from *Calyx* by permission of the author.

William Meredith. "Nixon's the One" copyright © 1975 by William Meredith and reprinted from *Hazard, the Painter* (Alfred A. Knopf). "Poem" copyright © 1980 by William Meredith, first appeared in *Inlet Magazine* and reprinted from *The Cheer* (Alfred A. Knopf). Both reprinted by permission of the author.

E. Ethelbert Miller. "Candy" copyright © 1995 by E. Ethelbert Miller. "Rebecca" copyright © 1994 by E. Ethelbert Miller and reprinted from *First Light: New and Selected Poems* (Black Classic Press). "Song for My Lady, or Excuse Me McCoy" copyright © 1982 by E. Ethelbert Miller, first published in *Season of Hunger/Cry of Rain* (Lotus Press) and reprinted from *First Light*. All reprinted by permission of the author.

May Miller. "Blazing Accusation," "They Knew It Was Christmas," and "The Tree House" copyright © 1989 by May Miller and reprinted from *Collected Poems* (Lotus Press).

Kathy Mitchell. "Needing To Dream" copyright © 1995 by Kathy Mitchell.

Miles David Moore. "Full Moon on K Street" copyright © 1995 by Miles David Moore.

Elisabeth Murawski. "At the Sedona Cafe" copyright © 1990 by Elisabeth Murawski and reprinted from *Shenandoah: The Washington and Lee University Review*, with permission of the editor. "Driving on Empty" copyright © 1993 by Elisabeth Murawski and reprinted from *Poetry Northwest*, with the permission of the editor.

Sharon Negri. "The Muse Checked Out Last Week" copyright © 1992 by Sharon Negri and reprinted from *Metropolitain*. "The Other Woman" copyright © 1992 by Sharon Negri and reprinted from *The Monacacy Valley Review*. Both reprinted by permission of the author.

Jean Nordhaus. "Tell Me Color" copyright © 1979 by Jean Nordhaus, first published in *Chowder Review* and reprinted from *A Bracelet of Lies* (WWPH, 1987). "The Weekly Loaf" copyright © 1993 by The Modern Poetry Association, first appeared in *Poetry* and is reprinted by permission of the Editor of *Poetry*. Both reprinted by permission of the author.

John O'Dell. "Eating Snow" copyright © 1992 by John O'Dell and reprinted from *Painting at Night* (Little Cove Press) by permission of the author.

Betty Parry. "Late at Night," "The Promise," and "Visit To The Cemetery" copyright © 1994 by Betty Parry and reprinted from *Shake the Parrot Cage* (The New Poets Series) by permission of the author.

Alicia Partnoy. "Comunicación/Communication," "De exilio y amargura/Exile and Bitterness," and "Instantánea/Snapshot" copyright © by Alicia Partnoy and reprinted from *Revenge of the Apple/Venganza de la manzana* (Cleis Press) by permission of the author. English translations by Richard Schaaf, Regina Kreger, and Alicia Partnoy.

Linda Pastan. "Home for Thanksgiving," "Pears," and "Petit Dejeuner" copyright © 1980 by Linda Pastan and reprinted from *Setting the Table* (Dryad Press) by permission of the author.

Richard Peabody. "The Forgiveness Device" copyright © 1994 by Richard Peabody, first appeared in *The Pearl #12* and reprinted from *Buoyancy and Other Myths* (Gut Punch Press). "I'm in Love with the Morton Salt Girl" copyright © 1977 by Richard Peabody, first appeared in *Calvert Review* and reprinted from *I'm in Love with the Morton Salt Girl* (Paycock Press). Both reprinted by permission of the author.

Patric Pepper. "Lollygagging" copyright © 1995 by Patric Pepper.

Jennifer M. Pierson. "The important things" copyright © 1993 by Jennifer M. Pierson and reprinted from *Voices* by permission of the author.

Jacklyn W. Potter. "Groaning Bed" and "Menu" copyright © 1995 by Jacklyn W. Potter.

Mary Quattlebaum. "The Crush" copyright © 1995 by Mary Quattlebaum. "The Failing" copyright © 1993 by Mary Quattlebaum and reprinted from *The Denny Poems* (Lincoln College) by permission of the author.

Gretchen Primack. "Signs" copyright © 1995 by Gretchen Primack.

Beth Raps. "For You at Your Parents' House" copyright © 1995 by Beth Raps.

Heddy F. Reid. "Invitation to the Dance" and "New in Cartons" copyright © 1995 by Heddy F. Reid.

Elisavietta Ritchie. "Advice to a Daughter" copyright © 1995 by Elisavietta Ritchie. "Cacophonies" copyright © 1995. Both reprinted from *New York Quarterly* and *The Arc of the Storm* (Signal Books) by permission of the author.

Kim Roberts. "Maple" copyright © 1995 by Kim Roberts. "The Nameless" copyright © 1993 by Kim Roberts, first published in *Chattahoochee Review* and reprinted from *The Wishbone Galaxy* (WWPH) by permission of the author.

Maggie Rosen. "Enunciation" copyright © 1995 by Maggie Rosen.

Joe Ross. "ESTRANGED: kin" and "SENTIMENT: noise" copyright © 1995 by Joe Ross.

Natasha Sajé. "Appetites," "Leningrad," and "Spring Rolls" are reprinted from *Red Under the Skin*, by Natasha Sajé, by permission of the University of Pittsburgh Press. Copyright © 1994 by Natasha Sajé.

Robert Sargent. "Hannah" copyright © 1993 by Robert Sargent and reprinted from *South Dakota Review* by permission of the author.

Jane Schapiro. "Thigmotaxis" copyright © 1995 by Jane Schapiro and reprinted from *Tapping This Stone* (WWPH) by permission of the author.

Catherine Harnett Shaw. "The Redbud, the Maple and the Cherished Yard" copyright © 1983 by Catherine Harnett (Shaw) and reprinted from *Still Life* (WWPH) by permission of the author. "Want" copyright © 1995 by Catherine Harnett Shaw.

Stephen I. Shaw. "Nostalgia" copyright © 1995 by Stephen I. Shaw.

Myra Sklarew. "Interval" copyright © 1987 by Myra Sklarew and reprinted from *Altamira* (WWPH) by permission of the author. "Looking at Men" copyright © 1987 by Myra Sklarew and reprinted from *Like a Field Riddled by Ants* (Lost Roads Publishers) by permission of the author. "Toward Evening" copyright © 1995 by Myra Sklarew.

Susan Sonde. "American Gothic" and "Lone Pine" copyright © 1990 by Susan Sonde and reprinted from *BOMB* by permission of the author.

Isobel Routly Stewart. "After Death" copyright © 1982 by *American Poetry Association* and reprinted from *Wide Open Magazine* by permission of the author.

Bradley R. Strahan. "Touch" copyright © 1995 by Bradley R. Strahan.

Sylvana R. Straw. "dear Mark" copyright © 1995 by Sylvana R. Straw.

Laurie Stroblas. "Bodies of Water" and "Daylight Savings" copyright © 1995 by Laurie Stroblas.

Elizabeth Sullam. "Scarcity" copyright © 1995 by Elizabeth Sullam.

Henry Taylor. "Artichoke" copyright © 1985 by Henry Taylor. Reprinted from *The Flying Change* by permission of the author and Louisiana State University Press. "Bernard and Sarah" copyright © 1975, 1992 by Henry Taylor. Reprinted from *The Horse Show at Midnight* and *An Afternoon of Pocket Billiards* by permission of the author and Louisiana State University Press. "Remembering

Kevan MacKenzie" copyright © 1966, 1992 by Henry Taylor. Reprinted from *The Horse Show at Midnight* and *An Afternoon of Pocket Billiards* by permission of the author and Louisiana State University Press.

Joseph C. Thackery. "Blood Tie" copyright © 1989 by Joseph C. Thackery and reprinted from *Heartland Journal.* "Winter, 1933, Ohio" copyright © 1992 by Joseph C. Thackery and reprinted from *The Dark Above Mad River* (WWPH). Both reprinted by permission of the author.

Hilary Tham. "Grandfather's Favoritism" copyright © 1994 by Hilary Tham Goldberg and reprinted from *MEN & other strange myths* (Three Continents Press) by permission of the author.

Naomi Thiers. "I Have Hungered for the Flat Gold" and "Medelena" copyright © 1995 by Naomi Thiers.

Colette Thomas. "The Taming Power of the Great" copyright © 1995 by Colette Thomas.

Susan Tichy. "Woman Singing" copyright © 1995 by Susan Tichy.

Stacy Johnson Tuthill. "Sudanese Girl" copyright © 1995 by Stacy Johnson Tuthill.

Elaine M. Upton. "Now is the Time of Nostalgia," "oh be," and "What is a Poem? What is Home?" copyright © 1993 by Elaine M. Upton and reprinted from *Children of Apartness* (WWPH) by permission of the author.

Barrett Warner. "Hotel Baltimore" copyright © 1995 by Barrett Warner.

Margaret Weaver. "Greed" copyright © 1987 by Margaret Weaver and reprinted from *Blue Unicorn* by permission of the author.

Marie Pavlicek Wehrli. "Blood Thirst," "Khatum Speaks," and "Why We Do This" copyright © 1995 by Marie Pavlicek Wehrli.

Julia Wendell. "Food, Clouds, & Secrets" copyright © 1993 by Julia Wendell and reprinted from *Fires at Yellowstone* (The Bacchae Press) by permission of the author.

Reed Whittemore. "Clamming" copyright © Reed Whittemore and reprinted from *The Past, The Future, The Present* by permission of the author. "Today" copyright © 1995 by Reed Whittemore.

Br. Rick Wilson. "Time on its Side" copyright © 1987 by Br. Rick Wilson and reprinted from *The Other Side* by permission of the author.

Terence Winch. "Cathedral" copyright © 1992 by Terence Winch and reprinted from *The New Republic* by permission of the author.

Hastings Wyman, Jr. "December Trips and Dreams" copyright © Hastings Wyman, Jr., and reprinted from *Certain Patterns* (WWPH). "Spree" copyright © Hastings Wyman, Jr., appeared in *Cedar Rock, The Other Side of the Hill,* and *Certain Patterns.* Both reprinted by permission of the author.

Edwin Zimmerman. "Bulls" copyright © 1995 by Edwin Zimmerman.

We thank the following poets, from whose poems the section titles in this anthology are excerpted or adapted:

Food: What hunger first saw this as food, from "Artichoke," Henry Taylor. *Love: All we know of love,* from "Tarot Card IV. Emperor," Grace Cavalieri. *Sex: Flesh stirred to a touch,* from "She Remembers the First Time," Ann B. Knox. *Kinship: The place I started from,* from "Bernard and Sarah," Henry Taylor. *Loss: An unknown withered hour,* from "Groaning Bed," Jacklyn W. Potter. *Nostalgia: An undertow of dream and exile,* from "Nostalgia," Stephen I. Shaw. *Deprivation: Hunger waits with time on its side,* from "Time on its Side," Br. Rick Wilson. *Art: Raw chords ready for song,* from "The Muse Checked Out Last Week," Sharon Negri. *Physicality: How embrace my nakedness,* from "Rebecca," E. Ethelbert Miller. *Travel: Unexplained territories,* from "The Unexplained Territories," Geraldine Connolly. *Spirituality: Holy earth,* from "Toward Evening," Myra Sklarew. *Political and Otherwise: Besieged by want and want and want,* from "Superego Serenade," Barbara Goldberg. *Meaning: Puzzled by the missing constellations,* from "In the Nocturnal Animal House," Sarah Cotterill.

KARREN L. ALENIER is the author of two collections of poetry, *Wandering on the Outside* (The Word Works Press, 1975; reprinted 1979), and *The Dancer's Muse* (Ommation Press, 1981), and the editor of *Whose Woods These Are* (Word Works, 1983), an anthology of contemporary poetry. Winner of the Lincoln College Billee Murray Denny Award, Alenier has had poetry and fiction published in such journals as *Israel Horizons, Jewish Currents, The Crescent Review,* and *Mississippi Review.*

CICELY ANGLETON grew up in Minnesota and Arizona. She graduated from Vassar College and received her Ph.D. in medieval studies from Catholic University. She has given poetry readings at the 7 1/2 Club and Politics and Prose Bookstore, and her work has appeared in *Delos, Poet Lore,* and *Asha.*

BARRI ARMITAGE is the author of *Double Helix* (WWPH, 1993). She teaches poetry classes in Montgomery County, MD. Her poems have appeared in *Poetry, The Georgia Review, Prairie Schooner,* and *The Ohio Review,* with reprints in *The Anthology of Magazine Verse and Yearbook of American Poetry.*

MEL BELIN is an attorney and poet. Born and raised in Hazleton, PA, he received a B.A. in psychology at Dartmouth College, and a J.D. in law at George Washington University. His poems have appeared in numerous journals.

DAVID BRISTOL is a lawyer and author of two books of poetry, *Paradise and Cash* (WWPH, 1980), and *The Monk Who Made His Momma Happy* (The Bunny and the Crocodile Press, 1977).

LAURA BRYLAWSKI-MILLER was born and raised in Milan, Italy. She has published two books of poetry, *Luna Parks* (Fallon Press, 1980), and *The Snow on Lake Como* (WWPH, 1991), as well as literary essays and scientific articles. Brylawski-Miller holds an M.F.A. in creative writing, and is working at present on her second novel.

NANCY NAOMI CARLSON works as a guidance counselor at Springbrook High School in Montgomery County, MD. Her poems have appeared in such journals as *Antietam Review, The Bridge,* and *Wind.*

KENNETH CARROLL is a native Washingtonian and the father of a 12 year old. He is D.C. site coordinator for the WritersCorps Program and president of the African-American Writers Guild. His poetry, reviews, and articles have appeared in such anthologies as *Nommo, In Search of Color Everywhere,* and *Fast Talk, Full Volume,* and *The Washington Post* and *Black Arts Bulletin.* His first poetry volume, *So What,* is due out fall 1995.

GRACE CAVALIERI is the author of seven books of poetry, most recently *Poems: New and Selected.* She has had numerous plays produced, including two New York productions. She is the producer and host of the longstanding public radio program "The Poet and the Poem," which has been broadcast without interruption since 1977.

MAXINE CLAIR has an M.F.A. in creative writing and teaches at George Washington University. She is the recipient of a 1995 Guggenheim Fellowship. In addition to a poetry volume, *Coping With Gravity* (WWPH, 1988), she is the author of the award-winning short story collection *Rattlebone* (Farrar, Straus and Giroux).

WILLIAM CLAIRE started Washington's first small press in 1967, publishing and editing *Voyages: A National Literary Magazine* through its fifteenth and final issue in 1973. He has received a Rockefeller Foundation residency in Italy, edited *The Essays of Mark Van Doren, 1924–1972,* and has countless poems and essays in such publications as *The*

Nation, The New Republic, and *The New York Times*.

SHIRLEY G. COCHRANE is the author of two books of poetry, *Family and Other Strangers* (Word Works, 1986), and *Burnsite* (WWPH, 1979), as well as a book of memoirs, *Everything That's All* (Signal Books, 1991). She lives in Washington, D.C.

DON COLBURN is a reporter for *The Washington Post* and has an M.F.A. from Warren Wilson College. He won the D.C. Commission on the Arts and Humanities' Larry Neal Award in 1991 and the Discovery/ *The Nation* Poetry Award in 1993. His poems have appeared in *The Iowa Review*, *Ploughshares*, and *Virginia Quarterly Review*.

GAIL COLLINS-RANADIVE received an M.F.A. from The American University in 1988 and has taught at Georgetown University as well as at AU. She is the author of *Writing Re-creatively, A Spiritual Quest for Women*. Currently in seminary at Starr King School for the Ministry (Unitarian Universalist), she teaches a course entitled "Toward a Thealogy of Writing."

MAXINE COMBS has published a poetry chapbook, *Swimming Out of the Collective Unconscious* (Wineberry Press, 1989), a fiction chapbook, *The Foam of Perilous Seas* (Slough Press, 1990), and a full-length fiction collection, *Handbook of the Strange* (Signal Books, 1995). She teaches English at the University of the District of Columbia.

CHRISTOPHER CONLON spent three years in Africa as a Peace Corps volunteer. He recently completed an M.A. in American literature at the University of Maryland. Conlon's poems have appeared in *Wind*, *Negative Capability*, *America*, *The Thomas Wolfe Review*, and other journals.

GERALDINE CONNOLLY's work has appeared recently in *Poetry*, *West Branch*, and *The Plum Review*, as well

as the anthology, *Bless Me, Father* (Penguin Books, 1994). Her book *Food for the Winter* was published by Purdue University Press, and she has held fellowships from the National Endowment for the Arts, Yaddo and the Maryland State Arts Council.

SARAH COTTERILL is the author of *In the Nocturnal Animal House* (Purdue University Press, 1991). She teaches at The Writer's Center in Bethesda. She has received grants from the Maryland State Arts Council and the National Endowment for the Arts.

KATHERINE COTTLE's poems have appeared in *The Maryland Poetry Review*, *Willow Springs*, *The Greensboro Review*, *Blue Mesa Review*, and *So To Speak*. In the spring of 1994 she received an Academy of American Poets award. She resides in Phoenix, MD.

R.F. COYNE was educated at St. Louis University, Marquette University, and the Washington Theological Union. Coyne's poems, essays, and book reviews have appeared in *Rye Bread*, *The Laurel Review*, *Writers Exchange*, *Universitas*, and elsewhere.

MARY ANN DALY is writing a collection of poems based on souvenir postcards and a study of apparitions of the Virgin Mary in the United States. She is a photographer as well as a writer, and runs a phone system and teaches computer applications at Resources for the Future.

ANN DARR has published eight books of poetry, including *St. Ann's Gut* (William Morrow & Co., 1971), *Do You Take This Woman...* (WWPH, 1986), and *Flying the Zuni Mountains* (Forest Woods Media Productions, 1994). Born in Iowa, she wrote radio scripts in New York City and flew for the Army Air Force during World War II. She has taught at The American University since 1981. From 1976 through 1989 she was poet in residence with the Floating Center for the Arts, a summer traveling performance aboard the boat *Point Counter Point II* with the American Wind Symphony Orchestra.

DONNA DENIZÉ is a teacher of English at St. Albans School for Boys in Washington, D.C. She is a graduate of Howard University and Stonehill College. In 1986, she received grants to attend the Bread Loaf School of English, Lincoln College at Oxford University, and the Johns Hopkins Summer Writers' Conference.

WILLIAM DERGE's poems have appeared in *Croton Review*, *Berkeley Poet's Cooperative*, *hitchhiker*, *Aura*, and *Artful Dodge*, among others. He has also published articles in *The Washington Post* and *The Baltimore Sun*. He is a teacher in Gaithersburg, MD, where he lives with his wife and three children.

TOI DERRICOTTE has published three collections of poetry, *Natural Birth* (Crossing Press, 1983), *The Empress of the Death House* (Lotus Press, 1978), and *Captivity* (University of Pittsburgh Press, 1992). She is the recipient of two NEA fellowships, a Pushcart Prize, the United Black Artists Distinguished Pioneer of the Arts Award, and the Columbia Book Award. She is Associate Professor of English at the University of Pittsburgh and resides in Maryland.

NEAL MICHAEL DWYER studied poetry at the University of Nice and George Mason University. He is Associate Professor of English and French at Charles County Community College in Maryland, and his poems have been published in journals in the United States and France.

PAUL ESTAVER is author of the poetry volume, *Salisbury Beach—1954* (WWPH, 1983), and the novel *His Third, Her Second* (SoHo Press, 1989). He has received the Virginia Prize for Fiction and an NEA fellowship for poetry. Estaver

currently writes memoranda for the federal government.

ROLAND FLINT is a professor of English at Georgetown University. His poetry volumes include *Resuming Green* (The Dial Press), *Pigeon* (North Carolina Wesleyan Press), and *Stubborn* (University of Illinois Press). He is the current poet laureate of Maryland.

ELIZABETH FOLLIN-JONES's poetry has appeared in *Embers*, *The Pennsylvania Review*, *Passager*, and other journals. A short story of hers was a PEN Syndicated Fiction winner. Her chapbook, *One Flight from the Bottom*, won the Artscape Literary Arts Award in 1990.

LILLIAN FRANKEL is the author of 17 published juvenile books. She has edited children's magazines, and has written many humorous essays for the Style Plus section of *The Washington Post*. Frankel is the recipient of a poet-in-education grant from the Maryland State Arts Council.

NAN FRY is the author of *Relearning the Dark* (WWPH, 1991), and a chapbook of riddles translated from the Anglo Saxon entitled *Say What I am Called* (Sibyl-Child Press, 1988). She teaches in the academic studies department at the Corcoran School of Art in Washington, D.C.

MARTIN GALVIN is on the writing faculty at Walt Whitman High School and at The Writer's Center. His poems have appeared recently in *Four Quarters*, *Poet & Critic*, and *Poetry*, and he was the winner of the 1990 *Poet Lore* Narrative Poetry Contest. His volume of poetry, *Wild Card* (WWPH, 1989), won the Columbia Book Award, judged by Howard Nemerov.

PATRICIA G. GARFINKEL is the author of two collections of poetry, *Ram's Horn* (Window Press, 1980), and *From the Red Eye of Jupiter* (WWPH, 1990), and edited an anthology of poems by homeless adults, *Cool Fire* (Word Works,

1989). She has published poems in *Seattle Review*, *California Quarterly*, *Pittsburgh Quarterly*, *Science 83*, *Negative Capability*, *New Scientist*, *Hollins Critic*, and other journals.

HOWARD GOFREED is a computer systems application developer, one-time lawyer, and sometime poet. He coordinates the Autumn in Arlington Poetry Series at the Arlington Arts Center.

SID GOLD hails from New York City. He teaches or has taught writing at George Washington University, the University of Maryland, Bowie State University, and other area schools. He received first prize in the 1986 California Poetry Society contest.

BARBARA GOLDBERG is the author of four books, most recently, *Marvelous Pursuits*, winner of the Violet Reed Haas Award, Snake Nation Press, 1995. The recipient of two NEA fellowships, she is currently director of editorial services for the American Speech-Language-Hearing Association.

JAMES GRIFFIN was born in New York City, and has worked as a journalist, political campaign manager, government spokesman, and freelance writer. His poetry has appeared in *The Midwest Quarterly*, *Poet Lore*, and *The Monocacy Valley Review*, as well as several anthologies.

PAUL R. HAENEL, a native of Pittsburgh, received a B.A. in English from Pennsylvania State University and spent four years as a German linguist with U.S. Army intelligence. His volume of poetry, *Farewell, Goodbye, Wave Goodbye*, was published by WWPH in 1994. He works for Dean Witter Reynolds, Inc.

HAMOD (a.k.a. Sam Hamod) received a Ph.D. from the Writers' Workshop of the University of Iowa and has published eight books of poems, including *Dying with the Wrong Name* (Anthe/Smyrna Press). He is included in the anthology *Unsettling America* (Penguin/Viking, 1994). Hamod is on the faculty of Howard University.

JUDITH HARRIS is the author of *Poppies* (WWPH, 1981), and *Song of the Moon* (Orchises Press). Her poetry and essays have appeared in *Antioch Review*, *Boulevard*, *American Scholar*, *Midwest Quarterly*, *Tikkun*, and *The Women's Review of Books*. She teaches at George Washington University.

CLARINDA HARRISS lives in Baltimore. Her most recent books of poetry are *The Night Parrot* (Salmon Publishing, Galway, Ireland), and *License Renewal for the Blind* (winner of the 1994 American Chapbook Award, Cooper House, OK). She teaches English at Towson State University and runs the New Poets Series, Maryland's oldest continuously publishing small press.

RICHARD HARTEIS's latest book, *Keeping Heart: New and Selected Poems*, was published in 1994 by Orpheus House. He maintains his certification as a physician assistant and has worked as a teacher, radio producer, and project director for Westinghouse Electric Corporation.

REUBEN JACKSON's first book of poems, *fingering the keys* (Gut Punch Press) won the 1992 Columbia Book Award from The Poetry Committee of Greater Washington. He is also a music critic who pines over the beauty present in the Miles Davis/Gil Evans collaborations.

JOSEPHINE JACOBSEN was born in Canada of American parents. She has published seven books of poetry, two books of criticism with William R. Mueller, and three collections of short fiction. She was inducted into the American Academy of Arts and Letters in 1994.

PHILIP K. JASON teaches literature and creative writing at the U.S. Naval Academy in Annapolis. Co-editor of *Poet Lore* and workshop leader at The

Writer's Center, he is the author of ten books, including two collections of poetry from Dryad Press and a new volume, *The Separation*, from Burning Cities Press.

ROD JELLEMA began writing poetry in mid-career as a teacher of literature at the University of Maryland. He is the author of three books of poems including *The Eighth Day: New and Selected Poems* (Dryad Press). His books of translations include the bilingual volume, *The Sound That Remains, A Historical Collection of Frisian Poetry*. Jellema was the first director of the University of Maryland's creative writing program.

DAN JOHNSON has published *Suggestions from the Border* (State Street Press, 1983), *Glance West* (Sedwick House, 1989), and *Come Looking* (WWPH, 1995). He works in the wildlife department of the National Audubon Society.

JOY JONES, when not under the spell of a saxophone, writes poetry, plays, and essays. Her poems have appeared in the *WPFW 89.3 FM Poetry Anthology* (The Bunny and the Crocodile Press, 1992), *Bad Beats, Sacred Rhythms* (The Spoken Word, 1993), and in *The African American Review*.

BETH BARUCH JOSELOW is the author of five books of poetry, including *Gypsies* (WWPH, 1979), and *excontemporary* (Story Line Press, 1994). A playwright whose work has been produced in Washington and New York, she is also the author of two non-fiction books and winner of five grants from the D.C. Commission on the Arts and Humanities.

THOMAS M. KIRLIN co-authored with his wife the *Smithsonian Folklife Cookbook* (Smithsonian Press, 1991), which documents 25 years of the Festival of American Folklife on the Mall through photos, oral histories, and recipes. He received a Larry Neal writers award for poetry in 1988.

PETER KLAPPERT's books include *Lugging Vegetables to Nantucket* (winner of the Yale Series of Younger Poets, 1971), *Circular Stairs, Distress in the Mirrors* (Griffin, 1975), *The Idiot Princess of the Last Dynasty* (Knopf, 1984), and *'52 Pick-Up: Scenes from The Conspiracy, a Documentary* (Orchises Press, 1984). He teaches poetry in the M.F.A. program at George Mason University.

ANN B. KNOX's poems have appeared recently in *Poetry, Poets On:, Nimrod*, and other journals. She is an editor of *Antietam Review* and teaches at The Writer's Center. Knox is the author of a book of poetry, *Stonecrop* (WWPH, 1988), and a book of short fiction, *Late Summer Break* (Papier-Mache Press, 1995).

CAROLYN KREITER-FORONDA has more than 200 publications to her credit, including two poetry books, articles on writing, interviews, book reviews, and newspaper articles. In 1991 she was named a Virginia Cultural Laureate for her contributions to American literature. She previously published under the name, Carolyn Kreiter-Kurylo.

KWELISMITH is a jazz vocalist, poet, performance artist, and music educator. She has a poetry collection entitled *Slavesong: the art of singing* (Anacostia Repertory Co., 1989), and in 1992 WWPH issued her poems on audio tape, *Browngirl in the ring*. Kwelismith has performed and taught in museums, art spaces, and schools in the metropolitan area and is now completing "Secret Meeting," an African approach to music for young singers.

DAVID LANIER is a family physician from Washington, D.C., who recently recieved an M.F.A. degree from Warren Wilson College. Poems of his have appeared in *Poet Lore, The Louisville Review*, and the anthology

Articulations: The Body and Illness in Poetry (University of Iowa Press, 1994).

MARY ANN LARKIN teaches writing at Howard University. She is the author of *The Coil of the Skin* (WWPH, 1982), and her poems appear regularly in magazines and anthologies. She belongs to The Capitol Hill Poetry Group and co-founded the Big Mama Poetry Troupe.

BARBARA F. LEFCOWITZ is a writer and visual artist. She has published four books of poetry, including *The Queen of Lost Baggage* (WWPH, 1986), and a novel. Her poems, stories, articles, and reviews have appeared in over 100 journals, and she is the recipient of an NEA fellowship in poetry as well as fellowships from The Rockefeller Foundation and the Maryland State Arts Council.

MERRILL LEFFLER is the author of *Partly Pandemonium, Partly Love* and *Late Afternoon Light* (due out in 1995). He edited *The Changing Orders: Poetry from Israel* and is the publisher and editor of Dryad Press. Leffler is an environmental and science writer with the Maryland Sea Grant Program, University of Maryland.

ELLEN MAUCK LESSY, a clinical social worker, received a B.A. from William & Mary, an M.S. from Johns Hopkins, and an M.S.W. from Catholic University. Her poetry has appeared in *Rhino*, *The Reston Review*, and *The New Press Literary Quarterly*. She is a wife and the mother of three teen-aged daughters.

LYN LIFSHIN's numerous collections include *Black Apples*, *Upstate Madonna*, *Kiss the Skin Off*, *Not Made of Glass*, and *The Marilyn Monroe Poems* (Quiet Lion Press). She has edited four anthologies of women's writing including *Ariadne's Thread* (Harper and Row) and *Tangled Vines* (Beacon Press; enlarged edition re-published by Harcourt Brace Jovanovich). She is the subject of a documentary film, *Lyn Lifshin: Not Made of Glass*.

CARMEN LUPTON's poems have been published in *Cathay* and in *Mondo Barbie* (St. Martin's Press, 1993). She has read at the Miller Cabin Series.

MARIQUITA MacMANUS resides in Washington, D.C., and has published poems in *Webster Review*, *America*, *The Christian Science Monitor*, *Visions*, *The Plains Poetry Journal*, *Piedmont Literary Review*, and other journals.

ELAINE MAGARRELL teaches creative writing in the Washington, D.C., public schools. She is the author of two books of poems: *On Hogback Mountain* (WWPH, 1985), and *Blameless Lives*, Word Works Washington Prize winner, 1991.

VENETA MASSON is a family nurse practitioner as well as a poet and essayist. She is the author of *Just Who* (Crossroad Health Ministry, Inc., 1993), a collection of poems accompanied by photographs by James Hall.

DAVID McALEAVEY teaches English at George Washington University. He is the author of *Holding Obsidian* (WWPH, 1985), and three other books of poetry. He has edited an anthology of work by Washington writers, *Evidence of Community* (Center for Washington Area Studies at George Washington University, 1984), and a collection of essays, *Washington and Washington Writers* (Center for Washington Area Studies, 1986).

RICHARD McCANN is the author of *Nights of 1990* (Warm Spring Press, 1994), and *Ghost Letters* (Alice James Books, 1994), which received the 1994 Beatrice Hawley Award and a Capricorn Poetry Award. His work has appeared in such magazines and anthologies as *The Atlantic*, *Esquire*, *The Nation*, *The Penguin Book of Gay Short Stories*, and *Poets for Life: 76*

Poets Respond to AIDS. A former Jenny McKean Moore Writer-in-Washington, he now co-directs the graduate program in creative writing at The American University.

EUGENE J. McCARTHY, a native of Watkins, MN, represented Minnesota's Fourth District in the U.S. House of Representatives for 10 years. In 1958, and again in 1964, he was elected U.S. Senator from Minnesota. Since leaving the Senate, McCarthy has taught university courses in politics, literature, and history. He is the author of over a dozen books on various topics, including government and politics, foreign policy, children's stories, poetry, and satire. His most recent book is *Required Reading: A Decade of Political Wit and Wisdom.*

JUDITH McCOMBS's poems appear in *Calyx, Feminist Studies, Free State, Poetry, River Styx,* and *Sisters of the Earth.* Her recent books include *Against Nature: Wilderness Poems* (Dustbooks) and *20/20 Visionary Eclipse* (Wineberry Press).

WILLIAM MEREDITH's latest book, *Effort at Speech* (Orpheus House) features selected poems from *Partial Accounts* (Random House, 1987), which won the Pulitzer Prize for Poetry in 1989. In 1980 he won Bulgaria's highest literary prize, the Vaptsarov Award. Meredith taught for 40 years at Connecticut College, and served as Poetry Consultant to the Library of Congress.

E. ETHELBERT MILLER is the poetry editor for *The African American Review.* He is a board member of the PEN/Faulkner Foundation and the director of the African American Resource Center at Howard University. His most recent collection of poetry is *First Light: New and Selected Poems* (Black Classic Press, 1994). He is also the editor of the anthology *In Search of Color Everywhere* (Stewart Tabori & Chang, 1994).

MAY MILLER was born in Washington at the turn of the century and grew up in the Howard University community. She is the author of nine collections of poems, most recently, *Collected Poems* (Lotus Press, 1989). She collaborated on two volumes of plays, and her poems have appeared in *The Antioch Review, Callaloo,* and *Poetry,* among other journals. May Miller died in the winter of 1995.

KATHY MITCHELL is a freelance writer from Bluemont, VA. As a mid-life student, she received George Mason University's Anonymous Bosch Poetry Award in 1992 and 1993, and GMU's Virginia Downs Poetry Award in 1994. She submits to pastoral romanticism and formal compulsions.

MILES DAVID MOORE is a Washington correspondent for Crain Communications, Inc. He was twice a Jenny McKean Moore scholar at George Washington University, and performed at the 1993 National Poetry Slam in San Francisco. His poems have appeared in *New York Quarterly, Pivot,* and other magazines.

ELISABETH MURAWSKI works as a training specialist for the U.S. Census Bureau and is an adjunct professor at the University of Virginia's Academic Center in Falls Church, VA. She is the author of *Moon and Mercury* (WWPH, 1990). Murawski is the recipient of four grants from The Helene Wurlitzer Foundation, and her poems have appeared in *Grand Street, Poetry Northwest, Shenandoah,* and other journals.

SHARON NEGRI's poetry has appeared in *Antietam Review, Lip Service, The Monacacy Valley Review, Permafrost,* and *Rolling Stone,* among other publications. She is the author of *The Other Side of Now* (WWPH, 1989).

JEAN NORDHAUS has served as president of Washington Writers' Publishing House and Coordinator of Poetry Programs at the Folger

Shakespeare Library. Her second book of poems, *My Life in Hiding*, appeared in *Quarterly Review of Literature* in 1991.

JOHN O'DELL is from Annapolis and teaches French and English in Prince George's County, MD. His poems have appeared in *Ruby*, *The George Mason Review*, *Snake Nation Review*, and *The South Florida Poetry Review*, among others. He is the author of *Painting at Night* (Little Cove Press,1992).

BETTY PARRY founded the Textile Museum Poetry and Literature Series, and edited *The Unicorn and the Garden* (Word Works, 1978), an anthology based on that series. *In the Shadow of the Capitol*, her study of segregated Washington's African-American community, documents the rich heritage of the forerunners of modern black advocacy. Her most recent publication is a book of poems, *Shake the Parrot Cage* (The New Poets Series, 1994).

ALICIA PARTNOY came to exile in the United States after three years as a political prisoner in her native Argentina. She edited *You Can't Drown the Fire: Latin American Women Writing in Exile* (Cleis Press, 1988), and is author of the bilingual poetry chapbook, *Revenge of the Apple/Venganza de la manzana*. Partnoy now runs Cleis Press and lives in Washington, D.C., with her family.

LINDA PASTAN's numerous poetry collections include *An Early Afterlife, PM/AM, New and Selected Poems* (Norton and Co.), *Heroes in Disguise, Waiting for My Life*, and *The Five Stages of Grief*. A longtime faculty member at the Bread Loaf Writers' Conference, she has received NEA fellowships and has served as poet laureate of Maryland.

RICHARD PEABODY edited *Gargoyle* magazine from 1976 to 1990. He is co-editor of the *Mondo Barbie* (1993), *Mondo Elvis* (1994),

and *Mondo Marilyn* (1995) anthologies, published by St. Martin's Press, and *Coming to Terms: A Literary Response to Abortion* (The New Press, 1994). His fourth book of poems is *Bouyancy and Other Myths* (Gut Punch Press, 1995).

PATRIC PEPPER is a manufacturing engineer. His poetry has appeared in *Hiram Poetry Review, Eclectic Literary Forum, Poetpourri, Plains Poetry Journal, Wind, Piedmont Literary Review*, and elsewhere. He received honorable mention in the 1993 Chester H. Jones Foundation National Poetry Competition.

JENNIFER M. PIERSON lives in Washington, D.C., and is passionate about vegetables, books, alleyways, and liberal ideals. Her favorite contemporary poet is Li-Young Lee. She is prone to exaggeration but continues to believe in Harvey, the great white rabbit.

JACKLYN W. POTTER's poetry and translations have appeared in anthologies and journals such as *If I Had My Life to Live Over, I'd Pick More Daisies* (Papier-Mache Press, 1992), *The Washington Review*, and *Journey Proud: Southern Women's Writings* (Carolina Wren Press, 1994). In 1994, *Delos, A Magazine on Translation*, featured her interview with Richard Harteis and William Meredith on their Bulgarian poetry translations. For the past 11 years, Potter has served as director of the Joachin Miller Cabin Series.

GRETCHEN PRIMACK is a writer and labor organizer. A graduate of Oberlin College, she has been published in *Exit 13, The Riverwest Review*, and *The Suffering Whitebread Anthology*. With the help of dogs, tofu, and some breathers out in the wilderness, Primack hopes to unionize as much of the U.S. workforce as possible in her lifetime.

MARY QUATTLEBAUM directs Arts Project Renaissance, a creative writing program for older adults in

Washington, D.C. She is the author of five children's books published or forthcoming from Bantam Doubleday Dell, including *Jackson Jones and the Puddle of Thorns* (1994). Her poems have appeared recently in *The Gettysburg Review* and *The Formalist*.

BETH RAPS tries to be as soulful in her work as a fundraising consultant as in her poetry. She is the translator of two anthropological works from French, both published by the University of Chicago Press.

HEDDY F. REID is a freelance writer and editor who has lived in Washington for over 25 years.

ELISAVIETTA RITCHIE is the author of *Flying Time: Stories and Half-Stories, The Arc of the Storm, Elegy for the Other Woman, A Wound-Up Cat and Other Bedtime Stories, Raking the Snow,* and *Tightening the Circle of Eel Country.* She is the editor of *The Dolphin's Arc: Endangered Creatures of the Sea.*

KIM ROBERTS is the author of *The Wishbone Galaxy* (WWPH, 1994). Her poems have appeared widely in journals throughout the United States, Canada, and Ireland. She is the recipient of grants from the D.C. Commission on the Arts and Humanities, the National Endowment for the Humanities, and eight writer's residencies at five artist colonies.

RON RODRIGUEZ authored *The Captains That Dogs Aren't,* one of WWPH's earliest publications. His first literary inspirations were The Three Stooges, who taught him how to speak English. Over the years, his influences have included Salvador Dali, Charlie Parker, and Buddhism. He studied with Allen Ginsberg and William Burroughs at the Naropa Institute.

MAGGIE ROSEN teaches English as a Second Language, and has worked as an editor and writer specializing in education. Her poetry has appeared

in *Old Hickory Review* and *Intuitions.*

JOE ROSS is literary editor of *The Washington Review,* president of the board of The Poetry Committee of Greater Washington, and co-coordinator of the In Your Ear Poetry Series at the District of Columbia Arts Center. Ross is the author of eight books of poetry, including *EQUATIONS=equals* (Sun & Moon Press, 1995), *An American Voyage* (Sun & Moon, 1993), and *Guards of the Heart* (Sun & Moon, 1990).

NATASHA SAJÉ's book of poems, *Red Under the Skin,* won the Agnes Lynch Starrett Prize and was published by the University of Pittsburgh Press in 1994. She is completing a Ph.D. in English at the University of Maryland and lives in Baltimore.

ROBERT SARGENT has published five books of poetry: *Now is Always the Miraculous Time* (WWPH, 1977), *A Woman from Memphis* (Word Works, 1979; reprinted 1981 and 1988), *Aspects of a Southern Story* (Word Works, 1983; reprinted 1987), *Fish Galore* (The Bunny and the Crocodile Press, 1989), and *The Cartographer* (Forest Woods Media Productions, 1994).

JANE SCHAPIRO's poems have appeared in such journals as *The American Scholar, The Gettysburg Review,* and *Prairie Schooner.* WWPH published her collection, *Tapping This Stone,* in 1995. She has taught physical education, worked in Israel, and bicycled across the United States. Schapiro lives in Annandale, VA, with her husband and three daughters.

CATHERINE HARNETT SHAW has worked for the federal government since coming to Washington in 1976. She is the author of *Still Life* (WWPH, 1983), and has poems published or forthcoming in such journals as *Fine Madness, Gargoyle, Connecticut River Review, Yankee,* and *Chatahoochee Review.*

STEPHEN I. SHAW has published work in *The Cumberland Poetry Review*, *Green Fuse*, and other journals. He has studied poetry at the 92nd Street 'Y' in New York and at The Writer's Center in Bethesda.

MYRA SKLAREW teaches creative writing at The American University. She is the author of *Altamira* (WWPH, 1987), *Eating the White Earth* (poems translated by Moshe Dor, published in Hebrew in Israel in 1994), and *Lithuania: New and Selected Poems* (Azul Editions, 1995).

SUSAN SONDE is associate fiction editor of *Crescent Review*. Her stories and poems have appeared in *Carolina Quarterly*, *Kansas Quarterly*, *Southern Humanities Review*, *The Ohio Review*, and other journals. She is the author of two books of poetry, *In the Longboats with Others* (New Rivers Press, 1988), winner of the Capricorn Book Award, and *Inland is Parenthetical* (Dryad Press, 1979).

ISOBEL ROUTLY STEWART was born in Toronto, Canada. She has published under several names in the United States and Canada, including Toni Stewart and Toni Collins.

BRADLEY R. STRAHAN teaches poetry at Georgetown University and is the publisher of *Visions-International* and *Black Buzzard Review*. He is the author of several books of poetry and has published over 500 poems in journals such as *Cross-currents*, *America*, *The Christian Science Monitor*, *Confrontation*, *Onthebus*, *Sources* (Belgium), *Poetry Monthly*, *Shimunhak* (Korea), and *The Salmon* (Ireland).

SILVANA R. STRAW is a recipient of the Outstanding Women Poets award from Judith's Room in New York. She was the Washington, D.C., Poetry Slam Champion in 1993 and 1994 and has competed in two National Poetry Slams. She has also appeared in theatrical productions through Scena, The Source, Metrostage, and Poetry Theater.

LAURIE STROBLAS is an editor/writer and the founder of the District Lines Poetry on the Metro Project, which spotlights the poetry of Washington, D.C.'s youth on posters on the city's transit system. She has been an arts administration fellow at the NEA and poet-in-residence at Children's Hospital. In 1994 she served on the panel for the Mayor's Arts Awards.

ELIZABETH SULLAM was born in Italy and has published poems in Italy, the United States, and Canada. She is the author of a novel, *A Canossa*, published in Italy in 1995, and a book of poems, *Out of Bounds* (Scripta Humanistica, 1987).

HENRY TAYLOR is co-director of the M.F.A. program in creative writing at The American University. His books include *The Horse Show at Midnight* (Louisiana State University Press, 1966), *An Afternoon of Pocket Billiards* (University of Utah Press, 1975), and *The Flying Change* (LSU Press, 1985), which received the 1986 Pulitzer Prize for Poetry. His most recent book is a collection of essays, *Compulsory Figures* (LSU Press, 1992).

JOSEPH C. THACKERY is a retired attorney and former teacher of creative writing at The American University, from which he received the M.F.A. after 35 years as a government labor lawyer. He is the author of *The Dark Above Mad River* (WWPH, 1992), and his poems have appeared in *Attention Please*, *Lip Service*, *Atlanta Review*, and other journals.

HILARY THAM, a Chinese Malaysian poet, is the author of four books published in the United States: *Paper Boats* (Three Continents Press, 1987), *Bad Names for Women* (Word Works, 1989), *Tigerbone Wine* (Three Continents, 1992) and *MEN & other strange myths* (Three Continents, 1994). Her work has appeared in *Antietam Review*, *Metropolitan*, *Gargoyle*, *Visions*, and *Midstream*.

NAOMI THIERS is the author of *Only the Raw Hands Are Heaven* (WWPH, 1992). Her poems, stories, book reviews, and interviews have appeared in many journals and anthologies, and her poetry and fiction have been nominated for Pushcart Prizes. She is currently writing for associations, working on a novel, and raising a daughter.

COLETTE THOMAS is the recipient of an Academy of American Poets College Prize and several other poetry awards from Harvard University, where she studied with Seamus Heaney. Her poems have appeared in *Grand Street*, *Poet Lore*, *Zone 3*, and other magazines. She also lectures on the *I Ching* and teaches Taoist meditation.

SUSAN TICHY is the author of *The Hands in Exile* (Random House, 1983), and *A Smell of Burning Starts the Day* (Wesleyan University Press, 1988). Her awards include an NEA fellowship and publication in the National Poetry Series. She teaches in the writing program at George Mason University.

STACY JOHNSON TUTHILL is the author of *Pennyroyal* (SCOP Publications, 1991), poems about the Great Depression; a chapbook, *Necessary Madness* (University of Alaska, Fairbanks, 1992); and a book of fiction, *The Taste of Smoke: Stories About Africa* (East Coast Books, 1995).

ELAINE M. UPTON's *Children of Apartness* (WWPH, 1993), based on her experiences living in South Africa and the United States, was a co-winner of the Columbia Book Award from the Poetry Committee of Greater Washington and a finalist for the Paterson Poetry Prize. She teaches African and African-American literature at the University of Maryland.

BARRETT WARNER's poetry has appeared in *Turnstile*, *Obfuscating on Thin Ice*, *Shattered Wig Review*, *California Quarterly*, and *Berkeley Poetry Review*, among others. His chapbook is called *Til I'm Blue in the Face* (Tropos Press, 1995). He is a farm foreman at a thoroughbred nursery in West Howard County, MD.

MARGARET WEAVER is a retired teacher, a tree farmer, and a gardener who despairs of catalogue perfections. She has had poems published recently in *Passager* and *Poet Lore*.

MARIE PAVLICEK WEHRLI is a painter and printmaker who recently exhibited at the Westminster College Art Gallery in New Wilmington, PA. She has read her poetry at the Miller Cabin Series and lives with her husband and two sons.

JULIA WENDELL is the author of *An Otherwise Perfect History* (Ithaca House) and *Fires at Yellowstone* (The Bacchae Press). She has been editor-in-chief at The Galileo Press, Ltd., a literary small press, since its founding in 1980. She lives with her two children, John and Caitlin, a dog, two cats, a rabbit, some fish, a big pole in the yard, and a rented horse named Peanut.

REED WHITTEMORE has twice been the Poetry Consultant to the Library of Congress and was the poet laureate of Maryland. He is the author of 14 books of poetry and biography and is professor emeritus, University of Maryland. He has edited *Furioso*, *The Carleton Miscellany*, and *Delos, A Magazine on Translation*, and has been literary editor of *The New Republic*.

BR. RICK (DIDACUS) WILSON, T.O.R., is a Franciscan Brother, former high school teacher, and Ph.D. candidate in religion and literature and adjunct professor at Catholic University. He is the author of two poetry collections, *Off the Backroads* (Hard Cider Press, 1979), and *Between a Rock & a Hard Place* (Scripta Humanistica, 1987). His poems have appeared in periodicals and anthologies and he was the recipient of the David Lloyd Kreeger Literature Award for his poems in 1990.

TERENCE WINCH is author of the poetry volumes *The Great Indoors* (Story Line Press, 1995), and *Irish Musicians/American Friends*, which won an American Book Award. *Contenders* is his short story collection. In 1992 *Irish America* magazine selected Winch as one of the "Top 100 Irish Americans," recognizing his work with the traditional Irish band, Celtic Thunder.

HASTINGS WYMAN, JR., was born in Aiken, SC, in 1939. He has lived in Washington, D.C., since 1967. His work has appeared in a number of publications and anthologies. In 1982 WWPH published his book of poems, *Certain Patterns*.

EDWIN ZIMMERMAN's first published poem appeared in 1993 in *Partisan Review*. He is a member of the Folger Shakespeare Library's poetry board.